FIRST
WORD

LAST
WORD

GOD'S
WORD

Titles in the Seedbed Daily Text series:

The Seedbed Daily Text

FIRST WORD

LAST WORD

GOD'S WORD

The Bible

J. D. WALT

Scripture quotations are taken from the Holy Bible, New International Version®, NIV® Copyright © 1973, 1978, 1984, 2011 by Biblica, Inc.™ Used by permission of Zondervan. All rights reserved worldwide. www.zondervan.com The "NIV" and "New International Version" are trademarks registered in the United States Patent and Trademark Office by Biblica, Inc.™ All rights reserved worldwide.

Scripture quotations marked ESV are taken from the ESV® Bible (The Holy Bible, English Standard Version®), copyright © 2001 by Crossway, a publishing ministry of Good News Publishers. Used by permission. All rights reserved.

Scripture quotations marked MSG are taken from *THE MESSAGE*, copyright © 1993, 1994, 1995, 1996, 2000, 2001, 2002 by Eugene H. Peterson. Used by permission of NavPress. All rights reserved. Represented by Tyndale House Publishers, Inc.

Scripture quotations marked KJV are taken from the Holy Bible, King James Version, Cambridge, 1796.

Printed in the United States of America

Cover and page design by Strange Last Name
Page layout by PerfecType, Nashville, Tennessee

Walt, John David.
   First word, last word, God's word : the Bible / J.D. Walt. –
Franklin, Tennessee : Seedbed Publishing, ©2020.

        pages ; cm. – (Seedbed daily text)

        ISBN 9781628247930 (paperback)
        ISBN 9781628247947 (Mobi)
        ISBN 9781628247954 (ePub)
        ISBN 9781628247961 (uPDF)

        1. Bible--Evidences, authority, etc.--Meditations. 2. Bible—
        Inspiration--Mediations. 3. Spiritual exercises. I. Title. II. Series.

BS480.W34 2020   220.1/3   2020940079

SEEDBED PUBLISHING
Franklin, Tennessee
seedbed.com

Contents

CONTENTS

An Invitation to Awakening

This resource comes with an invitation.

The invitation is as simple as it is comprehensive. It is not an invitation to commit your life to this or that cause or to join an organization or to purchase another book. The invitation is this: to wake up to the life you always hoped was possible and the reason you were put on planet Earth.

It begins with following Jesus Christ. In case you are unaware, Jesus was born in the first century BCE into a poor family from Nazareth, a small village located in what is modern-day Israel. While his birth was associated with extraordinary phenomena, we know little about his childhood. At approximately thirty years of age, Jesus began a public mission of preaching, teaching, and healing throughout the region known as Galilee. His mission was characterized by miraculous signs and wonders; extravagant care of the poor and marginalized; and multiple unconventional claims about his own identity and purpose. In short, he claimed to be the incarnate Son of God with the mission and power to save people from sin, deliver them from death, and bring them into the now and eternal kingdom of God—on earth as it is in heaven.

In the spring of his thirty-third year, during the Jewish Passover celebration, Jesus was arrested by the religious authorities, put on trial in the middle of the night, and at their urging, sentenced to death by a Roman governor. On the day known to history as Good Friday, Jesus was crucified on a Roman cross. He was buried in a borrowed tomb. On the following Sunday, according to multiple eyewitness accounts, he was physically raised from the dead. He appeared to hundreds of people, taught his disciples, and prepared for what was to come.

Forty days after the resurrection, Jesus ascended bodily into the heavens where, according to the Bible, he sits at the right hand of God, as the Lord of heaven and earth. Ten days after his ascension, in a gathering of more than three thousand people on the Day of Pentecost, a Jewish day of celebration, something truly extraordinary happened. A loud and powerful wind swept over the people gathered. Pillars of what appeared to be fire descended upon the followers of Jesus. The Holy Spirit, the presence and power of God, filled the people, and the church was born. After this, the followers of Jesus went forth and began to do the very things Jesus did—preaching, teaching, and healing—planting churches and making disciples all over the world. Today, more than two thousand years later, the movement has reached us. This is the Great Awakening and it has never stopped.

Yes, two thousand years hence and more than two billion followers of Jesus later, this awakening movement of Jesus Christ and his church stands stronger than ever. Billions of ordinary people the world over have discovered in Jesus Christ an awakened life they never imagined possible. They have overcome challenges, defeated addictions, endured untenable hardships and suffering with unexplainable joy, and stared death in the face with the joyful confidence of eternal life. They have healed the sick, gathered the outcasts, embraced the oppressed, loved the poor, contended for justice, labored for peace, cared for the dying and, yes, even raised the dead.

We all face many challenges and problems. They are deeply personal, yet when joined together, they create enormous and complex chaos in the world, from our hearts to our homes to our churches and our cities. All of this chaos traces to two originating problems: sin and death. Sin, far beyond mere moral failure, describes the fundamental broken condition of every human being. Sin separates us from God and others, distorts and destroys our deepest identity as the image-bearers of God, and poses a fatal problem from which we cannot save ourselves. It results in an ever-diminishing quality of life and ultimately ends in eternal death. Because Jesus lived a life of sinless perfection, he is able to save us from sin and restore us to a right relationship with God, others, and ourselves. He did this through his sacrificial death on the cross on our behalf. Because Jesus rose from the dead, he is able to deliver us from death and bring us into a quality of life both eternal and unending.

This is the gospel of Jesus Christ: pardon from the penalty of sin, freedom from the power of sin, deliverance from the grip of death, and awakening to the supernatural empowerment of the Holy Spirit to live powerfully for the good of others and the glory of God. Jesus asks only that we acknowledge our broken selves as failed sinners, trust him as our Savior, and follow him as our Lord. Following Jesus does not mean an easy life; however, it does lead to a life of power and purpose, joy in the face of suffering, and profound, even world-changing, love for God and people.

All of this is admittedly a lot to take in. Remember, this is an invitation. Will you follow Jesus? Don't let the failings of his followers deter you. Come and see for yourself.

Here's a prayer to get you started:

> Our Father in heaven, it's me [say your name], I want to know you. I want to live an awakened life. I confess I am a sinner. I have failed myself, others, and you in many ways. I know you made me for a purpose and I want to fulfill that purpose with my one life. I want to follow Jesus Christ. Jesus, thank you for the gift of your life and death and resurrection and ascension on my behalf. I want to walk in relationship with you as Savior and Lord. Would you lead me into the full-ness and newness of life I was made for? I am ready to follow you. Come, Holy Spirit, and fill me with the love, power, and purposes of God. I pray these things by faith in the name of Jesus, amen.

It would be our privilege to help you get started and grow deeper in this awakened life of following Jesus. Visit seedbed.com/Awaken for some next steps and encouragements.

How the Daily Text Works

It seems obvious to say, but the Daily Text is written every day. Mostly it is written the day before it is scheduled to release online.

Before you read further, you are cordially invited to subscribe to and receive the daily e-mail. Visit seedbed.com/dailytext to get started. Also, check out the popular Facebook group, Seedbed Daily Text.

Eventually, the daily postings become part of a Daily Text discipleship resource. That's what you hold in your hands now.

It's not exactly a Bible study, though the Bible is both the source and subject. You will learn something about the Bible along the way: its history, context, original languages, and authors. The goal is not educational in nature, but transformational. Seedbed is more interested in folks knowing Jesus than knowing *about* Jesus.

To that end, each reading begins with the definitive inspiration of the Holy Spirit, the ongoing, unfolding text of Scripture. Following that is a short and, hopefully, substantive insight from the text and some aspect of its meaning. For insight to lead to deeper influence, we turn the text into prayer. Finally, influence must run its course toward impact. This is why we ask each other questions. These questions are not designed to elicit information but to crystallize intention.

Discipleship always leads from inspiration to intention and from attention to action.

Using the Daily Text as a Discipleship Curricular Resource for Groups

While Scripture always addresses us personally, it is not written to us individually. The content of Scripture cries out for a community to address. The Daily Text is made for discipleship in community. This resource can work in several different ways. It could be read like a traditional book, a few pages or chapters at a time. Though unadvisable, the readings could be crammed in on the night before the meeting. Keep in mind, the Daily Text is not called the Daily Text for kicks. We believe Scripture is worthy of our most focused and consistent attention. Every day. We all have misses, but let's make every day more than a noble aspiration. Let's make it our covenant with one another.

For Use with Bands

In our judgment, the best and highest use of the Daily Text is made through what we call banded discipleship. A band is a same-gender group of three to five people who read together, pray together, and meet together to become the love of God for one another and the world. With banded discipleship, the daily readings serve more as a common text for the band and grist for the interpersonal conversation mill between meetings. The band meeting is reserved for the specialized activities of high-bar discipleship.

To learn more about bands and banded discipleship, visit discipleshipbands.com. Be sure to download the free *Discipleship Bands: A Practical Field Guide* or order a supply of the printed booklets online. Also be sure to explore Discipleship Bands, our native app designed specifically for the practice of banded discipleship, in the App Store or Google Play.

For Use with Classes and Small Groups

The Daily Text has also proven to be a helpful discipleship resource for a variety of small groups, from community groups to Sunday school classes. Here are some suggested guidelines for deploying the Daily Text as a resource for a small group or class setting:

1. Hearing the Text

Invite the group to settle into silence for a period of no less than one and no more than five minutes. Ask an appointed person to keep time and to read the biblical text covering the period of days since the last group meeting. Allow at least one minute of silence following the reading of the text.

2. Responding to the Text

Invite anyone from the group to respond to the reading by answering these prompts: What did you hear? What did you see? What did you otherwise sense from the Lord?

3. Sharing Insights and Implications for Discipleship

Moving in an orderly rotation (or free-for-all), invite people to share insights and implications from the week's readings.

What did you find challenging, encouraging, provocative, comforting, invasive, inspiring, corrective, affirming, guiding, or warning? Allow group conversation to proceed at will. Limit to one sharing item per turn, with multiple rounds of discussion.

4. Shaping Intentions for Prayer

Invite each person in the group to share a single disciple-ship intention for the week ahead. It is helpful if the intention can also be framed as a question the group can use to check in from the prior week. At each person's turn, he or she is invited to share how their intention went during the previous week. The class or group can open and close their meeting according to their established patterns.

Introduction

It's one of my favorite stories in the Bible. The young boy, Samuel, slept in the house of the Lord, near the ark of the covenant. One night, God began calling out his name. "Samuel! Samuel!" He thought it was the priest Eli, so he went to Eli's room and responded. This happened two more times before Eli realized what was happening.

> Then Eli realized that the Lord was calling the boy. So Eli told Samuel, "Go and lie down, and if he calls you, say, 'Speak, Lord, for your servant is listening.'" So Samuel went and lay down in his place. (1 Sam. 3:8–9)

Samuel returned to his bed.

> The Lord came and stood there, calling as at the other times, "Samuel! Samuel!"
>
> Then Samuel said, "Speak, for your servant is listening." (v. 10)

And the rest, as they say, is history.

Something worth noting, however, is the sentence in the first verse of this story of Samuel's awakening.

> "In those days the word of the Lord was rare; there were not many visions." (v. 3:1b)

One of the great gifts of our modern age is that we have no shortage of Bibles. The Word of the Lord is not rare. Or is it? It is one thing for the Word of the Lord to be bound in our Bibles and yet another for the Word to be unleashed in our lives. That is the purpose of the Seedbed Daily Text and this book you hold in your hands (or see on your screen). Unless the Word of God be loosed from its binding, it remains just that—another book on our shelf or bedside table.

First Word. Last Word. God's Word. The point is to get the Word of God off of the pages and into our hearts; words enfleshed in our lives. Can we find ways to make God's Word the first word of our day and the last word of our day? As we invoke this kind of priority we will find the Spirit of God weaving the Word of God into the warp and woof of our everyday world.

This has always been the vision of God for his people. Consider this celebrated text from Deuteronomy, commanded by God as the people prepared to enter the promised land.

> "These commandments that I give you today are to be on your hearts. Impress them on your children. Talk about them when you sit at home and when you walk along the road, when you lie down and when you get up. Tie them as symbols on your hands and bind them on your foreheads. Write them on the doorframes of your houses and on your gates." (Deut. 6:6–9)

Throughout the Bible we see many texts like this one, which speak about the nature, character, and purpose of Scripture.

Many such texts are engaged in these pages. The book ends with a creedal kind of affirmation lifting out many of these elements. We decided to bring the affirmation forward and share it as we begin:

I believe in the living Word of God,
    who is the Son of God, Jesus Christ.

And I believe in the written Word of God, the Bible,
    the Holy Spirit–inspired authority of the people of God.

God's Word endures forever,
    is sweeter than honey,
    more precious than gold,
    sharper than a double-edged sword,
    judging the thoughts and attitudes of the heart.

This Word is perfect, trustworthy, right,
    radiant, pure, firm, and flawless.
It refreshes the soul,
    makes wise the simple,
    gives joy to the heart,
    is a lamp to my feet and a light to my path.

God's Word teaches, corrects, rebukes, and trains.
It cleanses and prunes, feeds and nourishes,
    is purposeful and powerful.
It burns like a fire in my bones.
It always accomplishes the purposes for which it is sent.

God's Word will be on my heart,
    on my gate, on my doorpost.
I will talk about it when I lie down and
    when I wake up and when I walk along the road.
I will read, ruminate, rememberize, research, and rehearse it,
    building my life on the rock of God's Word.
Indeed, "the grass withers and the flowers fall,
    but the word of our God endures forever."

It will be the first Word.
It will be the last Word.
This is God's Word.*

As we enter into this First Word—Last Word—God's Word journey, let us remember and take on the posture of young Samuel, attentive and attuned, ready and waiting with anticipation, *"Speak, for your servant is listening."*

---

*This poem is inspired by Scripture. See the following verses: John 1:1, 2 Timothy 3:16–17, Isaiah 40:8, Psalm 19:10, Hebrews 4:12, Psalm 19:7–9, Psalm 199:105, John 15:2–8, Isaiah 55:8–9, 11, Jeremiah 20:9, Deuteronomy 6:4–9.

First Word. Last Word. God's Word.

1

ISAIAH 40:8 | The grass withers and the flowers fall, but the word of our God endures forever.

Consider This

What are the two most important words of the day? I'm glad you asked. My take: the first word and the last word. Who gets the first word in your day? Who gets the last word?

I have a confession. In recent months, I have realized my slow drift into giving Instagram the first word of my day. It was simple and benign; just a quick scroll through the photos my friends posted over the last half day or so. Then this realization: Netflix was getting the last word of my day. Before drifting off to sleep I would watch the next episode of some show that had caught my attention along the way. First word: Instagram. Last word: Netflix.

Days become weeks. Weeks become months. Months become years. And days, weeks, months, and years become us. Our lives consist not in the big decisions and banner events dotting our calendars but in the little things we consistently do day after day after day. We are what we do . . . every single day.

Back to the two most important words of the day: the first word and the last word. Each one of us has within our stewardship the ability to decide who will get those words in our lives. You know where this is headed. But first let me tell you what happened with my Instagram-Netflix ways. The problem with me so often is the way I want to make Instagram and Netflix the problem, when they aren't the problem. The problem is with me and the misspent priority of my own heart. So I didn't decide to delete Instagram and swear off Netflix. Instead, I decided I would shift the priority of my heart. I determined to give the Word of God the first word and the last word of my days. More on that to come later.

Though my day may be filled with a thousand distractions and a hundred course corrections, it is now determined—my day will be framed, surrounded with, enclosed by the Word of God. First Word. Last Word. God's Word.

So with that setup, here's the First Word–Last Word text to begin with at any time, anywhere, on any occasion: *The grass withers and the flowers fall, but the word of our God endures forever.*

Consider the stark simplicity and brazen boldness of this word from the prophet Isaiah. Everything is ephemeral. Only one thing is eternal: the Word of God. Next to the front door of our home, the one we enter and exit through most every time, is a chalkboard. On the chalkboard are written these words: *The grass withers and the flowers fall, but the word of our God endures forever.* I read it at least once every single day. I say it aloud so my ears can hear it. Can I possibly be reminded enough that everything around me is passing away save one thing: the Word of God? Can I possibly be encouraged enough to build my life on the singular enduring reality of the Word of God? First Word. Last Word. God's Word.

This will be the point of the next twenty-seven days. Each day we will gather around a different text from somewhere across the Bible. The invitation will be to allow the Scripture text itself to speak both the first and the last word of our day. Write the text for the day in a journal, on a notecard, a white board, or a chalk board, and make it a simple act of worship each morning to read it aloud as the first Word of the day and to read it aloud at the close as the last Word of the day.

Along the way we will reflect together on how to increase the priority and prominence and woven-ness of the Word of God in our everyday lives. If we will give ourselves to the gentle work of this way of walking together, I suspect we will find pathways of delight and devotion winding through the wilderness of this world and the sanctuaries of our souls we never imagined existed. And something tells me these First Word–Last Word–God's Word paths will find their way into this month, the next month, and so on.

The Prayer

Our Father in heaven, thank you for your Word, which endures forever. Thank you for seeing that it was written down in a book that is available to us. Thank you for sending your Son, who brought this Word into human flesh, and thank you for your Spirit who would bring this Word into our own lives and breath and give us the substance of eternal endurance.

Open my mind and my heart to your Word like never before. We pray in the name of Jesus Christ, our Lord. Amen.

The Questions

- Are you ready for the First Word–Last Word–God's Word challenge? Will you really do it?

2 On the Most Important Subject and Curriculum of Our Lives

ISAIAH 55:10–11 | As the rain and the snow
    come down from heaven,
and do not return to it
    without watering the earth
and making it bud and flourish,
    so that it yields seed for the sower and bread for the eater,
so is my word that goes out from my mouth:
    It will not return to me empty,
but will accomplish what I desire
and achieve the purpose for which I sent it.

Consider This

Yesterday's text revealed the Word of God as an eternally enduring word. Today's text shows us it is an extraordinarily powerful word. We must, however, understand the nature and character of this power. It is not power in the way the world understands power as force or might. It is far more subtle and infinitely more profound. Let's back up two verses in this prolific chapter 55 for more context.

"For my thoughts are not your thoughts, neither are
your ways my ways," declares the LORD.
"As the heavens are higher than the earth,
so are my ways higher than your ways
and my thoughts than your thoughts." (vv. 8–9)

There is only one way we can possibly begin to grasp the thoughts and ways of the almighty God of heaven and earth. We cannot figure them out or discern them with our natural minds. They must be revealed to us. This is the miracle of the Word of God. He has revealed his thoughts and ways, his mind and heart, his intentions, purposes, and will to us through his revealed Word. We are finite, fallen, and frail human beings, created in God's image and yet irreparably broken apart from his mercy and grace. The thoughts and ways of the one whose image we bear are infinitely higher than ours. The good news is we have the revealed Word of God and through this revealed Word, by the power of his Spirit, God will show us his thoughts and ways in particular applications for our lives.

Now, a word about the nature and character of the power of this God and his Word. As I said, it is not power as the world understands power, and yet is power according to the way creation works. Read verse 10 of today's text again.

As the rain and the snow come down from heaven, and do not return to it without watering the earth and making it bud and flourish, so that it yields seed for the sower and bread for the eater,

There are, in fact, two books constantly revealing the nature and will of God, and we must have them both to walk with God according to his thoughts and ways. They are the book of creation and the book of revelation.

Here is a mysterious truth at the heart of the cosmos. The revealed Word of God creates, and the creation, in turn, reveals the nature and character of the Word of God. Revelation creates. Creation reveals. This is true of the stars and the sky and of our very lives. This interplay throughout all of Scripture is fascinating. When God wants to point aging Abraham and barren Sarah to the promise of their impossible family, he lifts their gaze to the galaxies. The creation is not a transactional metaphor in the mind of God, something he uses to teach us by simple analogy. The creation is a transcendent medium. (That's deep, I know, and I hardly even grasp it, but I'm learning with you as we go.) You get it. After all, this God sets wild bushes on fire without burning them up! By the end of this fifty-fifth chapter alone, look at what's happening in this transcendent, transformed place called earth:

"You will go out in joy and be led forth in peace; the mountains and hills will burst into song before you, and all the trees of the field will clap their hands." (v. 12)

And, yes, creation is fallen, but God is redeeming all of it, not just rescuing the people out of it. This is why he will ultimately send his Son, as the revealed Word of God made flesh, not just to save us but to redeem us, and he will send his Spirit to transform the whole kit and caboodle into the new creation.

Through it all, his Word is working. It's working like rain and snow falling on the ground, germinating the seed of his Word in the soil of our lives and causing the slow, steady growth into plant and flower and fruit for our provision and seed for our sowing as we join God in this transformational work.

So is my word that goes out from my mouth: It will not return to me empty, but will accomplish what I desire and achieve the purpose for which I sent it.

It is slow work. It is steady work. It is everyday work. And this because it is the unrivaled transformational, powerful work of Father, Son, and Holy Spirit. Which is why our horizons of understanding and acting on God's Word must be greatly expanded. We are behind, and yet we can still be right on time. God's Word will not fail . . . ever.

Let me adapt the old saying: "Question: When is the best time to start taking God at his Word? Answer: Twenty years ago." When is the second-best time? Today! Right now! The Word of God is the single most important subject and curriculum of our entire lives, and we must be given to it wholeheartedly and unreservedly for the rest of our days. His revelation recreates us, and this new creation reveals him.

First Word. Last Word. God's Word.

The Prayer

Our Father in heaven, thank you for your Word, which endures forever. Thank you for the way your revealed Word created the whole creation and how your creation continually reveals your glorious Word. Thank you for the Word made flesh and the new creation. And thank you for bringing this new creation into my very soul. I want to hunger for your Word and thirst for your Spirit. I open myself to more of you. I will awaken and arise according to your Word, every single day. You will be my First Word and my Last Word. We pray in the name of Jesus Christ, our Lord. Amen.

The Questions

- Will you write out Isaiah 55:10–11 in your notebook or on a card or somewhere with relative permanence right now? Will you speak it aloud tonight as the last word of your day and again in the morning as the first word?

3 Better than Money; Sweeter than Honey

PSALM 19:7–11 | The law of the Lord is perfect,
refreshing the soul.
The statutes of the Lord are trustworthy,
making wise the simple.

The precepts of the LORD are right,
  giving joy to the heart.
The commands of the LORD are radiant,
  giving light to the eyes.
The fear of the LORD is pure,
  enduring forever.
The decrees of the LORD are firm,
  and all of them are righteous.

They are more precious than gold,
  than much pure gold;
they are sweeter than honey,
  than honey from the honeycomb.
By them your servant is warned;
  in keeping them there is great reward.

Consider This

There are two more little foxes always ready to jump into the vineyard of our early mornings and late nights. They come in the form of delving into our e-mail inboxes and diving into our text-messaging apps. When we do this, we inevitably surrender the first word and last word of our days to the always urgent and rarely too important words of other people. E-mail and text messages can wait. You have the rest of the day for that. This is about cultivating the sacred priority: First Word. Last Word. God's Word.

Psalm 19 brings us a brilliant celebration of the beauty, blessings, and benefits of the Word of God. As with yesterday's text, we see the two books of God on grand display again today. Look how the psalmist unfolds the book of creation:

> The heavens declare the glory of God;
> the skies proclaim the work of his hands.
> Day after day they pour forth speech;
> night after night they reveal knowledge.
> They have no speech, they use no words;
> no sound is heard from them.
> Yet their voice goes out into all the earth,
> their words to the ends of the world.
> In the heavens God has pitched a tent for the sun.
> It is like a bridegroom coming out of his chamber,
> like a champion rejoicing to run his course.
> It rises at one end of the heavens
> and makes its circuit to the other;
> nothing is deprived of its warmth. (vv. 1–6)

And, in a move of seamless genius, the psalmist dives headlong into the glories of the book of Revelation:

The law of the Lord is perfect, refreshing the soul. The statutes of the Lord are trustworthy, making wise the simple. The precepts of the Lord are right, giving joy to the heart. The commands of the Lord are radiant, giving light to the eyes. The fear of the Lord is pure, enduring forever. The decrees of the Lord are firm, and all of them are righteous.

The Word of God is perfect, trustworthy, right, radiant, pure, and firm. It refreshes, makes wise, grants joy, gives light, endures forever, and brings righteousness. I want to be refreshed in my soul, wise in my mind, joyful in my heart, luminous in my vision, persevering in my spirit, and robed in the righteousness of God. You want these things too. The Spirit has just revealed the vast contents of a veritable treasure trove. Indeed, this is true prosperity, says the psalmist:

They are more precious than gold, than much pure gold; they are sweeter than honey, than honey from the honeycomb. By them your servant is warned; in keeping them there is great reward.

The way to this blessed life is clear. John Wesley may have put it best when he said, "God has written it down in a book. O give me that book. At any price, give me the book of God. I have it. Here is knowledge enough for me. Let me be *homo unius libri* [a man of one book]."

E-mail, text messages, or . . . First Word. Last Word. God's Word.

The Prayer

Our Father in heaven, thank you for your Word, which is more precious than gold and sweeter than honey. I desire to know this Word in a way beyond knowledge. I want to know this Word and, in knowing it, to know you. I want the wonder of your Word as well as the warning; the help of your Word as well as the holiness. I repent from my ever-present readiness to listen to so many words and neglect the priority of your Word. Forgive me and by your Spirit set me on this new path of First Word. Last Word. God's Word. We pray in the name of Jesus Christ, our Lord. Amen.

The Questions
- Are you shifting your priority from so many other words at the beginning and end of your day to First Word. Last Word. God's Word? Stay with it. It will take time to regroove the pattern.

4 To Live in a Word-Shaped World

DEUTERONOMY 6:4–9 | "Hear, O Israel: The LORD our God, the LORD is one. Love the LORD your God with all your heart and with all your soul and with all your strength. These commandments that I give you today are to be on your hearts. Impress them on your children. Talk about them when you sit at home and when you walk along the road, when you lie down and when you get up. Tie them as symbols on your hands and bind them on your foreheads. Write them on the doorframes of your houses and on your gates."

Consider This

Isn't this a little excessive or fanatical even? Who talks about the Word of God all the time? Who binds it to their hands and their foreheads and writes it on their doorframes and their gates?

Short answer: We do.

God created the creation by his Word. Humanity's failure to heed and obey God's Word wrecked the creation. God is now redeeming, restoring, and recreating the creation by his Word. This is the question we must constantly engage: Are we heeding and obeying God's Word? The answer to the question will be determined by how much of a reality Deuteronomy 6:4–9 is in our lives.

God knows how prone we are to forget his Word and, even if we remember, we so easily misconstrue or misapply it. Sometimes I wonder what might have happened had God's signal command in the garden of Eden been written on a sign and nailed to the tree of the knowledge of good and evil.

The point of today's text is not so much about posting the rules as it is about fostering a Word-shaped world. We want to cultivate a daily–when we get up–breakfast, lunch, supper–when we lie down–walking along the road–teaching our children–sharing with one another relationship with the Word of God and the God of this Word. In a world filled with distraction, we want to do everything we possibly can to hone our attention on Father, Son, and Holy Spirit. In case we missed seeing the Word on the gate, we will catch it on the doorpost. In case we missed seeing the Word bound to the hand of our neighbor, we will see it on his forehead.

Note how the instructions center around our faculties of attention—of hearing and seeing. We are instructed to speak these words and talk about them, which engages our listening. We are instructed to post the Word of God in conspicuous places so that our eyes will see them. Eyes to see and ears to hear. Notice also the instruction referencing these words being "on our hearts." The Word of God keeps our hearts soft and pliable in the hands of God.

Finally, note how all of this is connected to the beginning and the end of loving God with all of our heart, and our soul, and our strength, which is the core of the core of the core of it all. Today's text reveals to us the impossibility of loving God without loving God's Word. Everything we care about in life we have a way of making practical, of keeping it before us all the time. We don't tend to put our passions and priorities in partitioned compartments. They tend to color our whole lives. It makes it all the more absurd the way we tend to keep God's Word in its designated place, like a church service or an appointed quiet time. To be clear, these places are good, but the point of the text is to say there are no boundaries for the Word of God. The notion of sacred space and secular space is an absurdity to the Bible. No place is too sacred and no place too profane to warrant the witness of the Word of God.

The Word of God will not be bound. In truth, we must labor to loose it from the bindings of our sacred books. Deuteronomy 6 calls us to be practical in our intentions and imaginative in our creativity when it comes to crafting the Word-shaped world in which we live. Why? Because this Word endures forever. It never returns to him empty but always accomplishes the purposes for which he sent it (Isa. 55:11). It is more precious than gold and sweeter than honey (Ps. 19:10).

First Word. Last Word. God's Word.

The Prayer

Our Father in heaven, thank you for your Word, apart from which we would have no idea of who you are. Thank you for your Word which informs of your love for us and which inspires and makes practical our love for you. Show me how to release your Word from my small categories and sacred compartments. I want for my whole life to be invaded, informed, and inspired by your inspired Word. Lead me in new ways with your Word and along new paths of righteousness for your name's sake. We pray in the name of Jesus Christ, our Lord. Amen.

The Questions

- In what practical and even imaginative ways are you releasing the Word of God from its bookish bindings and posting it in your everyday life and world? What have you learned from others in this regard? What ideas come to mind that you might consider? Are you worried about being perceived as an overly religious person? Why?

On the Word of God as Our Food

5

MATTHEW 4:4 | Jesus answered, "It is written: 'Man shall not live on bread alone, but on every word that comes from the mouth of God.'"

Consider This

So familiar have many texts in Scripture become to us that we no longer hear or see them. Because we have heard them so many times we take our understanding of them for granted. We become immune to their import and, consequently, we neglect them in our work of disciple-making.

We need to be shaken awake with texts like today's. We desperately need to recover a kind of beginner's mind when it comes to familiar texts. Though texts do have a clear and limited meaning and can't be bent into new and novel interpretations, one's understanding of the Word of God with the help of the Spirit of God can be limitless. When it comes to the revealed Word of God, there is always more understanding to be grasped.

The context of today's text centers around what we know as the temptation of Jesus by Satan in the wilderness.

> Then Jesus was led by the Spirit into the wilderness to be tempted by the devil. After fasting forty days and forty nights, he was hungry. The tempter came to him and said, "If you are the Son of God, tell these stones to become bread." (Matt. 4:1–3)

This is not practice; Jesus is in the game. Up to this point, Jesus lived a life of practice. He grew up in wisdom and stature and favor with God and God's people (Luke 2:52). He read, heard, meditated on, memorized, studied, and enacted the Word of God hour by hour, day by day, week by week, month by month, and year by year. For thirty years Jesus lived out a Deuteronomy 6:4–9 life and lifestyle. The will of the Word of God wove his world together into a seamlessness between heaven and earth that shaped his mind and heart, formed his soul and spirit, and literally became his source and strength—his sword and shield. The text makes clear, Jesus' dependence on the Word of God did not rival that of food; it equaled it:

Jesus answered, "It is written: 'Man shall not live on bread alone, but on every word that comes from the mouth of God.'"

Is it any wonder he is known to history and eternity as the Word made flesh? When the test came he was ready.

In essence, Jesus prepared thirty years for a three-year work. Oh, what difference it could make if we would consider preparing three years for what could be a thirty-year work! Still yet we see a deeper lesson in the life of our most-high mentor. For Jesus, practice was playing and playing was practice. All of life served as the playing field.

To be continued . . .

The Prayer

Our Father in heaven, thank you for your Word, which is not *like* food but is, in fact, food. Bring us into this kind of dependence on your Word until our dependence becomes our delight. I do not live by bread alone but on every word that comes from the mouth of God. Make it so through the strength of your indwelling Spirit. In the process, expose the junk-food habits of my soul and give me the will to amend my diet. We pray in the name of Jesus Christ, our Lord. Amen.

The Questions

- How is your own longing and desire for a Word-shaped life growing as we proceed on this journey together? Is your soul growing hungry? If so, this is a gift of God. Rejoice and reflect on that.

6 The Great Epiphany of the Word of God

JEREMIAH 15:16 | When your words came, I ate them;
  they were my joy and my heart's delight,
for I bear your name,
  Lord God Almighty.

Consider This

Let's reflect on Jesus' response to Satan's temptation in the wilderness: "It is written: 'Man shall not live on bread alone, but on every word that comes from the mouth of God'" (Matt. 4:4).

Let's take a closer look at the particular temptation to which he responded: "If you are the Son of God, tell these stones to become bread" (Matt 4:3).

This temptation, common to us all, goes straight for our core identity. It is the temptation to validate one's being by one's doing; to establish a sense of self and worth built around one's performance or one's appearance or some other self-generated manifestation of one's value. This is the essence of insecurity because no matter how much security we can amass for ourselves through our doings, it will never be enough to validate or legitimate our being.

Let's back up with a bit more context for our understanding. Prior to the Spirit's leading Jesus into the wilderness, he led him to the baptism in the Jordan River. As Jesus came up out of the water, the Spirit descended on him in the form of a dove and these words came directly from the mouth of God: "This is my Son, whom I love; with him I am well pleased" (Matt. 3:17).

In this light, remember Jesus' response to Satan's temptation: "It is written: 'Man shall not live on bread alone, but on every word that comes from the mouth of God'" (Matt. 4:4).

For forty days of fasting in the trackless wild, Jesus feasted on this word just spoken *from the mouth of God*: "My son. My beloved. With you I am well pleased" (author's paraphrase). These words came prior to any performance. They gave validation at the level of his deepest being as the beloved Son of an adoring Father.

This is the baptismal word of the Father over all who would follow his Son; a blessing word so many of us have never fully received and appropriated in our lives. As a result, we have labored and striven to merit our own worth, to earn our approval, and to prove our own value. So many now still strive with a hopeful optimism that at the end of their days they will hear him say, "Well done good and faithful servant!" (Matt. 25:21, 23). The gospel truth? He gives you the evaluation before the job even begins: "My son. My daughter. My beloved.

With you I am well pleased." It has nothing to do with your performance and everything to do with his pleasure in you. It brings us to the text for today from the prophet Jeremiah:

When your words came, I ate them; they were my joy and my heart's delight, for I bear your name, Lord God Almighty.

Herein lies a deep challenge for our inmost being. The Word of God must shift from a duty we perform to a desire in which we delight. In fact, this is a work God must do within us. He will do it by his Word and Spirit.

For the past twenty years, I have engaged in a daily practice based on Deuteronomy 6:4–9. It happens in the morning when I am in the shower (a baptismal environment no less). I speak these blessing words aloud over my own life as though being spoken by God. I speak my name, saying, "John David, you are my son. You are my beloved. With you I am well pleased." And I simply try to hear them with my ears. These words, simply spoken and faithfully heard, have changed me in the deepest way. These words drown out the lies I am so prone to believe about myself, and they remind me of the truth that sets me free. I have come to desire and delight in these words, and they have opened my soul to so many others in their wake. This has been, for me, the great epiphany of the Word of God in my own life. It unfolds more and more every single day. I commend the practice to you.

The Prayer

Our Father in heaven, thank you for your Word, which endures forever. I confess, it can be a duty to stay committed to daily engagement with Scripture. I don't want your Word to be my duty, but rather to be my desire and my delight. Come, Holy Spirit, and invade my inmost being with this kind of transforming work. I want your Word and your Spirit to be my deepest joy. Open my heart and mind to this new creation reality. We pray in the name of Jesus Christ, our Lord. Amen.

The Question

- Imagine a continuum on which the far left represents drudgery, in the middle is duty, and on the far right is delight. Where are you right now on that continuum in your relationship with the Word of God? Determine not where you want to be, but where you actually are, for God can only meet us where we are.

Learning to Listen to the Word of God

7

ISAIAH 55:1–3 | "Come, all you who are thirsty,
    come to the waters;
 and you who have no money,
    come, buy and eat!
Come, buy wine and milk
    without money and without cost.
Why spend money on what is not bread,
    and your labor on what does not satisfy?

Listen, listen to me, and eat what is good,
  and you will delight in the richest of fare.
Give ear and come to me;
  listen, that you may live.
I will make an everlasting covenant with you,
  my faithful love promised to David."

Consider This

For the next five entries we will share in a series of practical ways of engaging the Word of God in the power of the Spirit of God. Let's identify these words from this prophecy of Isaiah 55:3 as our First Word–Last Word text for today:

"Give ear and come to me; listen, that you may live."

The first key practice for engaging the Word of God is also the most overlooked one: hearing. This may surprise you, but the Word of God was not written to be read. It was written to be heard. At the time of its revelation there were no printing presses; only scrolls (and before that, stone tablets). People gathered in order to hear the Word of God. They heeded words from God like these of the prophet Isaiah:

"Give ear and come to me; listen, that you may live."

Reading is good, but reading has a way of bypassing our faculties of hearing. Reading leads to thinking and processing, but not to listening and hearing. Reading simply can't be the measure of engagement with God's Word because, for the overwhelming majority of human history, most people could not read. We are born hearing and seeing, not reading and thinking. Remember, also, we walk by faith and not by sight, and faith comes by hearing. Listening and hearing invoke our imagination, which lead to vision and seeing.

"Give ear and come to me; listen, that you may live."

Am I suggesting that we should only hear the Word of God? No. I am and will be insisting on all manner of engagement with God's Word. Listening and hearing are a good starting place. How do we do this? For starters, let's acknowledge that hearing takes at least two people; one to read aloud and the other to listen. This amplifies the preference of God to engage with us in our togetherness. If you are reading devotionally and in solitude, try reading aloud. Remember, the Word of God has power. There is no sweeter sound in any language than the audible sound of the spoken Word of God. It always accomplishes the purposes for which God sends it.

"Give ear and come to me; listen, that you may live."

Ask your children or grandchildren to read God's Word aloud to you. Read it aloud for them. A lot of worship services these days have all but dispensed with the reading of God's Word. If you are a preacher or worship leader, create space for the reading of Scripture in the midst of public worship.

"Give ear and come to me; listen, that you may live."

One of my First Word–Last Word practices each day for the past weeks engages my phone. Just before I turn off the light at night and the first thing I do in the morning is open the YouVersion Bible app and turn to the Psalms. Next, I click on the audio version and (at night) set the sleep timer for ten minutes. I focus on listening and usually drift off to sleep before it is finished. I try to cover ten psalms a day between the morning and night practices. In this way, I cover the entire 150 psalms twice per month. Already, this is changing me.

"Give ear and come to me; listen, that you may live."

First Word. Last Word. God's Word.

The Prayer

Our Father in heaven, thank you for your Word, which endures forever. Thank you for speaking your Word and inviting us to hear it. Thank you for this invitation to "Give ear and come to me," and to "listen" so that we might live. Open our ears in a way that your Word goes straight to our heart and, from there, let it become enfleshed in our lives. Come, Holy Spirit, and empower this good and delightful work with your Word. We pray in the name of Jesus Christ, our Lord. Amen.

The Question

- How will you engage this delightful work of listening to the Word of God?

8 Learning to Meditate on the Word of God

Psalm 1:1–3 ESV | Blessed is the man
    who walks not in the counsel of the wicked,
  nor stands in the way of sinners,
    nor sits in the seat of scoffers;

but his delight is in the law of the Lord,
   and on his law he meditates day and night.

He is like a tree
   planted by streams of water
that yields its fruit in its season,
   and its leaf does not wither.
In all that he does, he prospers.

Consider This

Yesterday we introduced the first formative, Spirit-empowered practice of engaging the Word of God: reading, and, more properly, hearing the Word of God. Today we take on the second practice: meditating.

Because of my propensity to engage in all manner of mnemonic and alliterative devices, by the time we are done with this exercise we will have five practices, each of which begin with the letter R and which also correspond with one's five fingers. Let's begin with the First Word–Last Word–God's Word portion of today's text from Psalm 1:2:

but his delight is in the law of the Lord, and on his law he meditates day and night.

Meditation is definitely in vogue these days. All the cool kids are doing it; however, before we go any further we need to establish the difference between the Bible's idea of meditation and the kind of meditation getting so much attention currently. While meditation is common to many religious traditions, there is a clear distinction with biblical meditation. Most common conceptions of meditation involve the attempt to empty one's mind of all things distracting and enter into a state of relaxation or higher consciousness. Meditation, in the biblical sense, is actually just the opposite. It means to fill one's consciousness with the Word of God; to relish and even devour it with deep delight.

but his delight is in the law of the LORD, and on his law he meditates day and night.

The Hebrew term behind the English term *meditate* in Psalm 1 offers the word picture of a lion hovering over the carcass of an animal it has caught with a growling delight over its deliciousness. I love to watch our little dog with a meaty bone. Lucy (short for Lucinda or Lucifer, depending on the day) loves to meditate. First, she takes the bone off to a quiet and relatively private place where she can meditate without distraction. After a good hour of getting every shred of anything resembling meat off the bone, she will take it out in the yard where she hides it for later. Later she will retrieve the bone, bring it back into the house, and continue gnawing on the bone until she breaks into the marrow. This is interspersed with interludes in which she will hide the bone again so she can reapproach it later. Little by little, the bone disappears until completely consumed and incarnated in her fifteen-pound Chihuahua–Jack Russell–and-only-God-knows-what else frame.

but his delight is in the law of the LORD, and on his law he meditates day and night.

Take the example, inserting yourself as Lucy and the Word of God as the bone and we have a brilliant image of biblical meditation. So, what is the R-word for meditate? Thanks for asking. How about *ruminate*? Cows ruminate. They have four different stomachs which involve a digestive process in which they swallow food, digest it a bit, and then regurgitate it back into their mouth in the form of a cud that they then chew on more, extracting more goodness. They ruminate. I love this example because of the ongoing processing nature of it. It is happening all the time and over the course of a long period of time. Cows are always grazing, always digesting, and, consequently, always ruminating. In this light, note the precise description given in the text for when we meditate or ruminate:

but his delight is in the law of the Lord, and on his law he meditates day and night.

It can't be compartmentalized into a tidy little practice we tuck between coffee and breakfast. It doesn't even let us off with our First Word–Last Word–God's Word practice. The psalmist reveals the time for meditation as "day and night." In other words, it gets back to the Deuteronomy 6:4–9 all-in-all-the-time mentality. Finally, notice in verse 3 how delighting in the Word of God leads to the deepest desire of our hearts in its outcome:

He is like a tree planted by streams of water that yields its fruit in its season, and its leaf does not wither. In all that he does, he prospers.

First Word. Last Word. God's Word.

The Prayer

Our Father in heaven, thank you for your Word, which endures forever. It is more precious than gold and sweeter than honey and always accomplishes the purposes for which you send it. Cultivate in me a deep delight in your Word. Train the taste buds of my spirit to savor your Word, to meditate and ruminate on it continuously. This feels challenging and even overwhelming to me, so grant me a humble start or a gracious next step on the journey. We pray in the name of Jesus Christ, our Lord. Amen.

The Questions

- How can you make a small start or take a next step with this practice of rumination (biblical meditation)? How might this coincide with the First Word–Last Word practice we are cultivating?

9 | Learning to Rememberize the Word of God

PSALM 119:11 | I have hidden your word in my heart that I might not sin against you.

Consider This

We began these five formative, Spirit-empowered practices for engaging the Word of God with reading (hearing).

Yesterday we covered rumination (meditating). Today we turn to our next practice which we find in Psalm 119:11, our First Word–Last Word text for the day:

I have hidden your word in my heart that I might not sin against you.

The R-word (and third finger from our mnemonic device) is *rememberize.* I know. It's not actually a word, but this practice is so distinctive that it merited the invention of a new word altogether. Perhaps you think I mean to say memorize. I don't. Let me tell you the story of the word's origin.

Years ago, when my oldest son, David, was four or five, we were working with him on memorizing Scripture. One day he rounded the corner into the kitchen with gleeful excitement and this announcement, "Mom! Dad! I finally rememberized it!" I've never forgotten that.

We all know what memorization means. It's that frenetic thing you do the night before a big exam in order to pass the test. We load in the information, and we pour it out on the paper and, in most cases, we promptly flush it into the nether regions of our skull or some other crevasse of our small intestines.

I have hidden your word in my heart that I might not sin against you.

Memorization quick-loads our short-term memory. Rememberization is of another order. It slow-loads our long-term memory. As an example, consider my grandmother (a.k.a. Meemaw), who had severe dementia for the last decade of her life. She could not remember who I was, but the minute I started praying the Lord's Prayer or saying the Apostles' Creed or singing "Tis So Sweet to Trust in Jesus," she was right there with me—every . . . single . . . word. This is because she was in church for some seventy years—every . . . single . . . Sunday . . . saying the Lord's Prayer and declaring the creed and singing the songs. She slow-loaded her long-term memory. She had rememberized it.

Maybe this is why the word "remember" is one of the most repeated and significant words in the whole Bible. To remember something is quite different than memorizing something. My Meemaw, and likely yours too, shows us how remembering actually survives complete memory loss. It's why there is no substitute for the long slow work of every day, every week, every month, every year, every decade. To remember something is to reattach to it in practical ways. Memorization is a brain activity; remembering requires soul-level engagement.

I have hidden your word in my heart that I might not sin against you.

I like how the English Standard Version translates this text from Psalm 119:11: "I have stored up your word in my heart, that I might not sin against you." This "storing up" comes from the Deuteronomy 6:4–9 every day–all the time–when I lay down–when I rise up–when I walk along the road–Word of God way of life.

So how do we rememberize? There are lots of ways. Let me share a practice I implemented with my children when they were young that continues to the present and which I also share in with friends on a daily and weekly basis now. I would like to call it texting, but that's kind of been taken now. Let's call it *versing*. I repeat the first half of a verse and the other person says the latter part.

> Me: I have hidden your word in my heart . . .
> Them: . . . that I might not sin against you.

I like to practice versing with text messaging. I text the first part (the call) and a friend texts back the rest (the response). Here are some more of my more recent go-to texts for versing.

> Me: My soul magnifies the Lord, . . .
> Them: . . . and my spirit rejoices in God my Savior.
>   (Luke 1:46 ESV)
> Me: Wake up, O sleeper, and rise from the dead, . . .
> Them: . . . and Christ will shine on you. (Eph. 5:14)
> Me: Oh, magnify the Lord with me, . . .
> Them: . . . and let us exalt his name together!
>   (Ps. 34:3 ESV)

Every morning on the way to school my youngest, Sam (age fourteen), and I do versing with Psalm 23 and, lately, with Proverbs 3:5–6.

I have hidden your word in my heart that I might not sin against you.

One last bit here. Note the purpose listed in Psalm 119:11: "that I might not sin against you." In this instance, the Hebrew word for *sin* means, "missing the mark." We tend to read this in a behavioral and moralistic framework (i.e., we hide God's Word in our heart to keep us from misbehaving). There is a better framing. We hide God's Word in our heart so we might hit the bull's-eye of the target for our lives. We hide God's Word in our heart so our lives will be filled with joy and resplendent with the glory of God. We hide God's Word in our heart because this is the one in whose image we are created and for whose purposes we are crafted.

I have hidden your word in my heart that I might not sin against you.

First Word. Last Word. God's Word.

The Prayer

Our Father in heaven, thank you for your Word, which endures forever. Thank you for this invitation to slow-load our long-term memory with your Word. I want to become a rememberizer. I love your Word, Lord. Help me hide it in my heart that I might not sin against you and even more so that my life might hit the bull's-eye of the target of your perfect will in all that I am and in all that I do. Lead me to those words you wish for me to store up in my heart and give me the day-by-day grace to do it. We pray in the name of Jesus Christ, our Lord. Amen.

The Questions

- How do you go about hiding God's Word in your heart? How will you? What are those everyday, slow-loading ways you have discovered along the path?

Learning to Study the Word of God

10

EZRA 7:10 | For Ezra had set his heart to study the Law of the LORD, and to do it and to teach his statutes and rules in Israel.

Consider This

We read God's Word. We ruminate on God's Word. We rememberize God's Word. Today we come to the fourth formative, Spirit-empowered way of engaging God's Word: study. The R-word is *research*.

The Bible is a complex book. In fact, it is sixty-six books. It was written on three different continents, in three different languages, by forty different authors, and over the period of some fifteen hundred years. Still, miracle of miracles, the Bible reveals a single, unifying, underlying, and overarching story. As has been said, the waters of Scripture are shallow enough for a baby to play in and yet deep enough for an elephant to drown. The Bible is the most significant and important book in the history of the world and is easily the best-selling book of all time.

What could be more worthy of our investment than a life-long study of the Word of God? It seems like a slam dunk. Sadly, it is not.

Johann Bengel, acclaimed eighteenth-century New Testament scholar, aptly wrote, "Apply yourself wholly to the text; apply the text wholly to yourself."* I would like to suggest that our involvement with Scripture does not begin with study. It begins with the kind of engagement identified so far. I see these practices of reading, rumination, remem-berization, and research as sequential. They describe, for me, a practical agenda for applying the whole of ourselves to the whole of the text. Listening and hearing the text, medi-tating and ruminating on it in our heart, and slow loading it into our mind for long-term memory feels like an embodied application of our whole selves to the Word of God.

So why not begin with studying God's Word? I like to think I am inviting the text to speak on its own terms to me. I want to hear the text in its native voice of revelation before I seek to mine it for its information. Scholars may disagree with me on this point and they may be right. I am not offering hard-and-fast rules here, but speaking from my sense of wisdom. This influences my choice of the term *research* over *study*. In my experience, study tends to be what I do when I want to master a body of knowledge. I do not mean this in any nega-tive sense. I do not view the Bible as a knowledge text, but as a wisdom text. I read the Bible in order to search for and grasp the wisdom of God.

As I am living with a text, the Spirit will spark my curiosity, which prompts me to research the text. Often I want to search out the context. I want to search out the meaning of original

---

*Johann Albrecht Bengal, quoted in the preface to his 1734 Greek New Testament.

Greek or Hebrew words using online tools. I want to understand where else in Scripture these words are used. I want to understand what saints and scholars have written about particular texts over the centuries. In doing this, it is critical to recognize and appreciate that we stand on the shoulders of giants. Were it not for faithful scholars digging deep wells into the biblical text for centuries, none of this would be possible. All of this helps in the task of applying the whole of myself to the whole of the text.

For Ezra had set his heart to study the Law of the LORD, and to do it and to teach his statutes and rules in Israel.

This is a good word about Ezra. Study it. Do it. And only then might we dare to stand and teach it.

First Word. Last Word. God's Word.

The Prayer

Our Father in heaven, thank you for your Word, which endures forever. Increase my appetite to search your Word and then to research it. Awaken my longing to drink deeply from the deep wells of the biblical text. Train me in searching more for wisdom than knowledge; that I may not seek to master the text but to be mastered by the God of the text. Show me what it looks like to apply the whole of myself to the whole of the text and the whole of the text to the whole of myself. All of this for my good and your glory. We pray in the name of Jesus Christ, our Lord. Amen.

The Questions

- Are you motivated to research the Word of God in new and deeper ways? What might that look like going forward for you? What is a practical step you can take? Where is your curiosity leading you? Start there.

11 Learning to Do the Word of God

JAMES 1:22–25 | Do not merely listen to the word, and so deceive yourselves. Do what it says. Anyone who listens to the word but does not do what it says is like someone who looks at his face in a mirror and, after looking at himself, goes away and immediately forgets what he looks like. But whoever looks intently into the perfect law that gives freedom, and continues in it—not forgetting what they have heard, but doing it—they will be blessed in what they do.

Consider This

We come to our fifth formative, Spirit-empowered way of engaging the Word of God. It comes from our First Word–Last Word text for today:

Do not merely listen to the word, and so deceive yourselves. Do what it says.

The R-word: *rehearse*. If we do not practice the Word of God all of our other engagements are for naught. Listen to the prescient words of Jesus on this same point from the celebrated Sermon on the Mount:

> *Therefore everyone who hears these words of mine and puts them into practice is like a wise man who built his house on the rock. The rain came down, the streams rose, and the winds blew and beat against that house; yet it did not fall, because it had its foundation on the rock. But everyone who hears these words of mine and does not put them into practice is like a foolish man who built his house on sand. The rain came down, the streams rose, and the winds blew and beat against that house, and it fell with a great crash.* (Matt. 7:24–27)

What is the difference between these persons? They both heard the Word of God. They both built houses. They both faced horrific storms. The only difference between the two people is one put the words of God into practice and the other did not. It made the difference between building on rock and building on sand.

Consider the mnemonic device of the five fingers. This fifth practice represents the thumb. Try picking something up without your thumb. The four fingers are rendered incompetent without a thumb. So it goes if we read, ruminate, rememberize, and research without rehearsing the Word of God. In fact, we engage the Word of God in all these ways in order that we might become better at doing what it says. Only when we actually do God's Word does it become enfleshed in our own lives. Only when we do God's Word can it become a blessing to others for their good and a witness to others of God's glory.

First Word. Last Word. God's Word.

The Prayer

Our Father in heaven, thank you for your Word, which endures forever. Thank you for not only calling me to be a doer of your Word, but for empowering me to do it by the power of your Spirit. I want to build my life on the rock of your Word. I confess that all my engagement with your Word is for naught lest I put it into practice in my life. Lead me in this everlasting way. We pray in the name of Jesus Christ, our Lord. Amen.

The Question

- What word from God are you presently working to put into practice in your life?

12 God-Breathed Words for a God-Breathed Life

2 TIMOTHY 3:16–17 | All Scripture is God-breathed and is useful for teaching, rebuking, correcting and training in righteousness, so that the servant of God may be thoroughly equipped for every good work.

Consider This

God-breathed. Did you catch that? *God-breathed.*

We live in a creation brought into being by God-breathed words. We are the image-bearers of God, those into whom God breathed the breath of life. And we know these things because we hold in our hands a book filled with God-breathed words:

All Scripture is God-breathed and is useful for teaching, rebuking, correcting and training in righteousness.

Are we awake to this revolutionary reality? All Scripture . . . every . . . single . . . word . . . breathed by God. Or have we slowly gone to sleep at the wheel, lulled into slumber by a doctrinaire confidence; no longer alert but aloof? There is only one way to know—a careful assessment of our level of engagement with this God-breathed book. Are we reading, ruminating, rememberizing, researching, and rehearsing the Word of God? Does this Word remain bound in our books or is it being liberated into our everyday walking around living and breathing lives? Are these words locked into the quiet-time compartments of our morning devotions or are we finding ways to loose them into the life-flow of the hours and minutes of our days and nights?

All Scripture is God-breathed and is useful for teaching, rebuking, correcting and training in righteousness.

I know. I know. Many of you feel as though you are doing well to read the Daily Text on most days. I appreciate this, and yet I am compelled to challenge you. As this series continues I intend to contend for more and more of your attention for the Word of God. Did you catch those four strategic words from today's text? *Teaching, rebuking, correcting,* and *training.* I tend to camp out around teaching and training, mostly steering clear of rebuking and correcting. I may foray into this more challenging territory in the days ahead. I love this word of rebuke and correction John Wesley gave to his preachers:

> Whether you like it or no, read and pray daily. It is for your life; there is no other way; else you will be a trifler all your days, and a petty, superficial preacher. Do justice to your own soul; give it time and means to grow. Do not starve yourself any longer. Take up your cross and be a Christian altogether. Then will all children of God rejoice (not grieve) over you in particular.*

We would be remiss not to note verse 17, which captures the purpose of this work of teaching, rebuking, correcting, and training in righteousness:

So that the servant of God may be thoroughly equipped for every good work.

It always comes back around to doing it. The test of discipleship is not discipline but devotion to doing it. The test of awakening is not waking up, as great as this is, but staying awake. This discipleship series aspires both to wake us up and to sustain the awakening. I want you and me to be thoroughly equipped for every good work.

---

*John Wesley to John Premboth on August 17, 1760. Quoted in Ben Witherington, *Is There a Doctor in the House? An Insider's Story and Advice on Becoming a Bible Scholar* (Grand Rapids: Zondervan, 2011), 71.

All Scripture is God-breathed and is useful for teaching, rebuking, correcting and training in righteousness.

First Word. Last Word. God's Word.

The Prayer

Our Father in heaven, thank you for your Word, which endures forever. Thank you for teaching, rebuking, correcting, and training me in righteousness. I want to be thoroughly equipped for every good work. I know it will not happen apart from your Word and your Spirit. Save me from self-congratulatory backslaps over baby steps. I need—no, I want—to be challenged to my core. We pray in the name of Jesus Christ, our Lord. Amen.

The Question

• When is the last time you found yourself rebuked or corrected by the Word of God?

The Word of God Is Alive and Active

13

HEBREWS 4:12 | For the word of God is alive and active. Sharper than any double-edged sword, it penetrates even to dividing soul and spirit, joints and marrow; it judges the thoughts and attitudes of the heart.

Consider This

Yesterday, we discussed the nature of Scripture as inspired, or God-breathed, and recounted the ways God's Word works to teach, rebuke, correct, and train us in righteousness. Today's text from Hebrews echoes and further elucidates these same ideas

For the word of God is alive and active.

As a publisher, it never ceases to amaze me just how quickly books age. Authors want the most recent copyright date possible. It is as though their words carry a life expectancy and it seemingly gets shorter and shorter every year. Most words don't age well. Sure, some authors' words carry more weight than others, and yet even the best authors with the best-selling books know once their words hit the page the clock starts ticking. I mean, no one seems to be talking much anymore about the phenomenal, best-selling book of only a few years ago, *The Purpose Driven Life*. Then, of course, there are the classics, aptly defined as books that everyone likes to talk about but no one actually reads.

All of these words we write, publish, and read are good, meaningful, insightful, helpful, and even powerful, and yet none of them make the claim Scripture makes concerning its words:

For the word of God is alive and active.

The Word of God is in a category all its own. Even among the world's collection of so-called holy books, nothing even comes close to rivaling the Holy Bible. Why? Because alive and active words can do things other words cannot:

Sharper than any double-edged sword, it penetrates even to dividing soul and spirit, joints and marrow.

This sword, like a surgical instrument, heals as it pierces, penetrates, and cuts out even the most malignant cancerous growths of sin and death in our inner being. Remember our foray into Psalm 19:11, where the psalmist noted, "by them [the Word of God] your servant is warned; in keeping them there is great reward." Our First Word–Last Word text for today concludes with this claim:

It judges the thoughts and attitudes of the heart.

This is good news. We do not have to judge the thoughts and attitudes of our own hearts or anyone else's. This is the purview of the Word of God. We do not need to be self-critical, just surrendered. Notice how the Word of God gets beneath behavior. A big part of our problem with sin is the way we try to battle it at the level of our behavior. Too often, by the time sin reaches our behavior, we have already lost the battle. The Word of God wills to intercede and intercept far before behavior and activity.

It judges the thoughts and attitudes of the heart.

All we need do is subject and submit our everyday, walking-around lives to this alive and active, sharper than any double-edged sword, mysterious, miraculous, and merciful Word of God: reading, ruminating, rememberizing, researching, and rehearsing. Consider the marvelous consonance of Hebrews 4:12 with Psalm 19:12–13:

> But who can discern their own errors?
>   Forgive my hidden faults.
> Keep your servant also from willful sins;
> may they not rule over me.
> Then I will be blameless,
> innocent of great transgression.

There is only one way this does not work, which is to absent ourselves from this wonder-working Word.

For the word of God is alive and active. Sharper than any double-edged sword, it penetrates even to dividing soul and spirit, joints and marrow; it judges the thoughts and attitudes of the heart.

First Word. Last Word. God's Word.

The Prayer

Our Father in heaven, thank you for your Word, which endures forever. Thank you that your Word is alive and active, sharper than any double-edged sword. Thank you for the precise way it cuts to the place where soul and spirit meet and mercifully judges the thoughts and attitudes of my heart. Give me grace to simply show up and surrender my deepest and inmost self to this amazing Word of God. We pray in the name of Jesus Christ, our Lord. Amen.

The Questions

- How have you and how are you experiencing the Word of God as this double-edged sword, mercifully judging the thoughts and attitudes of your heart? Do you tend to focus your energy at the level of behavior? Don't you want to engage at a deeper level? Now you know.

The Word of God Is Not Self-Help

14

JOHN 15:1–4 | "I am the true vine, and my Father is the gardener. He cuts off every branch in me that bears no fruit, while every branch that does bear fruit he prunes so that it will be even more fruitful. You are already clean because of the word I have spoken to you. Remain in me, as I also remain in you. No branch can bear fruit by itself; it must remain in the vine. Neither can you bear fruit unless you remain in me."

Consider This

The Word of God is inspired, or God-breathed. We learned yesterday how it is sharper than any double-edged sword, able to cut to the deepest place in our hearts; far beneath our behavior and into our dispositions, attitudes, and affections. Following Jesus often gets reduced to some dimension of behavior- (or sin-) management when, in reality, it is about the deep transformation of the heart and mind.

Today's text morphs the metaphor a bit from a sword to pruning shears. Note how Jesus begins by locating his hearers inside of the relationship he enjoys with his Father:

"I am the true vine, and my Father is the gardener."

Now, watch how he immediately cuts to the chase: "He cuts off every branch in me that bears no fruit, while every branch that does bear fruit he prunes so that it will be even more fruitful."

Did you catch how many branches are cut here? He cuts every branch that bears no fruit and every branch that does bear fruit. At last count, that was all of them: every . . . single . . . branch. The work of the Word of God to transform the image-bearers of God is not the exception but the rule. It is not occasional but comprehensive. In light of this, note the next word from Jesus to his disciples in verse 3. I would identify this as our First Word–Last Word for today:

"You are already clean because of the word I have spoken to you."

It is hard to overestimate the negative impact of the self-help industry on the Christian faith. Self-help inspires a take-charge, if-it-is-to-be-it-is-up-to-me, largely behavior-oriented, self-reliant approach to change. Don't hear me wrong; self has responsibility, but at the end of the day, self can't help. Note, Jesus did not say, "You are already clean because you have worked really, really hard to clean yourselves up." No. He said:

"You are already clean because of the word I have spoken to you."

What we need is far more engaging contact with the Word of God and Spirit of God and far less reliance on our own best change strategies, which is most often some combination of *The Little Engine That Could* and Dr. Phil. Self-help is seductive. It puts us in the driver's seat under the seemingly agreeable guise of taking personal responsibility for our lives. It creates an endless cycle of optimistic striving for an outcome we never seem to achieve. Self-improvement keeps the pruning shears in our own hands to do with as we see best. The problem is that we can't see best. Remember who does the pruning: "He cuts off every branch in me that bears no fruit, while every branch that does bear fruit he prunes so that it will be even more fruitful."

Now hear Jesus say it again:

"You are already clean because of the word I have spoken to you."

We are pruned, which is to say transformed, by the substance of the Word of God; not our own self-willed, take-charge efforts. It simply requires repeatedly showing up in surrendered submission and trusting obedience. Reading. Ruminating. Rememberizing. Researching. Rehearsing. (Rinse & Repeat). The Word of God must become the deep substance of our lives. He does not do his work through our working. This is the long, slow, steady path by which we learn the way to do our work through his working.

You are already clean because of the word I have spoken to you.

First Word. Last Word. God's Word.

The Prayer

Our Father in heaven, thank you for your Word, which endures forever. Thank you that it is not up to me to prune myself. Thank you that I need not strive to become all you desire for me; that, in fact, I will be transformed by exposure to and engagement with your Word and Spirit. Give me grace to simply show up and surrender my deepest and inmost self to this amazing Word of God. We pray in the name of Jesus Christ, our Lord. Amen.

The Questions

- Are you aware of the seductive strategies of self-help and self-improvement? And, particularly, how it keeps everything referenced around the self? Are you seeing how we need another point of reference?

15 First Word. Last Word. God's Word.—Midterm Review

PSALM 119:89 | Your word, Lord, is eternal;
it stands firm in the heavens.

Consider This

As we come to the halfway point in our First Word–Last Word–God's Word series, let's take a pause to review where we've been.

Only the Word of God endures forever.

The grass withers and the flowers fall, but the word of our God endures forever. (Isa. 40:8)

The Word of God is purposeful and powerful.

"So is my word that goes out from my mouth: It will not return to me empty, but will accomplish what I desire and achieve the purpose for which I sent it." (Isa. 55:11)

The Word of God is more precious than gold and sweeter than honey.

They are more precious than gold, than much pure gold;

they are sweeter than honey, than honey from the honeycomb.

By them your servant is warned; in keeping them there is great reward. (Ps. 19:10–11)

The Word of God creates and recreates the world of God.

"These commandments that I give you today are to be on your hearts. Impress them on your children. Talk about them when you sit at home and when you walk along the road, when you lie down and when you get up. Tie them as symbols on your hands and bind them on your foreheads.

Write them on the doorframes of your houses and on your gates." (Deut. 6:6–9)

The Word of God sustains us like food.
Jesus answered, "It is written: 'Man shall not live on bread alone, but on every word that comes from the mouth of God.'" (Matt. 4:4)

The Word of God is our joy and delight.
When your words came, I ate them; they were my joy and my heart's delight, for I bear your name, Lᴏʀᴅ God Almighty. (Jer. 15:16)

We read and listen to the Word of God.
"Give ear and come to me; listen, that you may live." (Isa. 55:3a)

We ruminate on the Word of God through meditation.
But his delight is in the law of the Lᴏʀᴅ, and on his law he meditates day and night. (Ps. 1:2 ESV)

We rememberize the Word of God.
I have hidden your word in my heart that I might not sin against you. (Ps. 119:11)

We research the Word of God.
For Ezra had set his heart to study the Law of the Lᴏʀᴅ, and to do it and to teach his statutes and rules in Israel. (Ezra 7:10 ESV)

We rehearse the Word of God.

Do not merely listen to the word, and so deceive your-selves. Do what it says. (James 1:22)

The Word of God teaches, rebukes, corrects, and trains us.

All Scripture is God-breathed and is useful for teaching, rebuking, correcting and training in righteousness, so that the servant of God may be thoroughly equipped for every good work. (2 Tim. 3:16–17)

The Word of God pierces and penetrates, shaping the thoughts and attitudes of the heart.

For the word of God is alive and active. Sharper than any double-edged sword, it penetrates even to dividing soul and spirit, joints and marrow; it judges the thoughts and attitudes of the heart. (Heb. 4:12)

The Word of God transforms us by pruning and cleansing us.

"You are already clean because of the word I have spoken to you." (John 15:3)

Your Word, LORD, is eternal; it stands firm in the heavens. (Ps. 119:89)

First Word. Last Word. God's Word.

The Prayer

Our Father in heaven, thank you for your Word, which endures forever, is purposeful and powerful, more precious than gold and sweeter than honey, is food for my life and a delight to my soul. Train me to read, ruminate, rememberize, research, and rehearse your unfailing Word. I welcome you to teach, rebuke, correct, and train me through your Word. I invite your Word to cut to the deepest place of my heart like a double-edged sword and transform me. I want your Word to prune and cleanse my deepest inmost self. Show me the practical ways your Word can order my steps, design my days, and constantly remind me of your grace and goodness. And all of this by your Spirit, Lord. We pray in the name of Jesus Christ, our Lord. Amen.

The Questions

- Where are you finding yourself most encouraged by this series so far? How about challenged? What is your single most important takeaway at the halfway point?

16 The Word of God and the Will of God

JOHN 15:7–8 | "If you remain in me and my words remain in you, ask whatever you wish, and it will be done for you. This is to my Father's glory, that you bear much fruit, showing yourselves to be my disciples."

Consider This

One of my first mentors in the Lord, Mrs. Betty Jane Oldner, always reminded me, "John David, you can't do the will of God

unless you know the Word of God." How does our engagement with God's Word impact our prayer life and pursuit of
God's will? Today's First Word–Last Word text gets at this:

*"If you remain in me and my words remain in you, ask what-
ever you wish, and it will be done for you."*

It is tempting to read this text at a transactional level. If I do
this, then God must do that. If I stay close to God and God's
Word, then he will have to do whatever I ask of him. I do my
part, and God does God's part. Something within our fallen
and broken humanity wants to hold a claim on God.

We must learn to read this text and, indeed, the whole of
the Word of God, at a transcendent level. At a transactional
level, we try and engage the Word of God on our terms and in
order to achieve our agenda; even what we might conceive of
as a godly agenda. At a transcendent level, we surrender our
lives to God and sign on to God's will and agenda in the world
(i.e., "on earth as it is in heaven" [Matt. 6:10]). We exchange
our control for an abiding relationship with Jesus. The reality
of abiding occurs as God's presence and plan transcends our
presence and plans.

*"If you remain in me and my words remain in you, ask what-
ever you wish, and it will be done for you."*

As the words of God remain or abide in us, the Spirit of
God transforms our heart and mind to reflect and refract
the heart and mind of Christ—indeed, the ways and will of
God—in our lives and relationships. We learn to pray the
kinds of prayers Jesus prays and that the Father answers. We
learn a way of praying that participates in the will of God as it

unfolds. We learn to pray simultaneously with humility and boldness, not presuming the outcome, but confident in God. In this way prayer ceases to be a transactional practice and becomes a transcendent place of laboring with God in the power of the Spirit for his will to be done. There is simply no way to get to this kind of place apart from a long, deep, and abiding engagement with the Word of God. The outcome of this kind of transcendent life is flourishing, fruit-bearing.

Hear Jesus on this point:

"This is to my Father's glory, that you bear much fruit, showing yourselves to be my disciples."

The transactional mentality understands the outcome of abiding to be receiving whatever we ask for in prayer. The transcendent mind-set understands the outcome of abiding to be bearing much fruit as the disciples of Jesus for the glory of the Father. As we abide in Jesus in the power of the Spirit and his words abide in us, our wishes come to be shaped by God's will, and their fulfillment becomes the great delight of God for the great good of his glory.

"If you remain in me and my words remain in you, ask whatever you wish, and it will be done for you. This is to my Father's glory, that you bear much fruit, showing yourselves to be my disciples."

First Word. Last Word. God's Word.

The Prayer

Lord Jesus, I want to abide in you and for your words to abide in me. I want this not for my agenda, but for your will to be done on earth as it is in heaven. I want for my prayers to be infused with the Word of God, for the Word to be encrypted and embedded in my praying. I want to learn to labor with you in prayer in the power of your Word and Spirit and not according to my willful pleadings and petitions. Train me in this way of life. I surrender myself completely to you and submit myself to your will and ways as I pray in your name, Jesus. Amen.

The Question
- How are you understanding this distinction being drawn between transactional faith and transcendent faith?

Growing Trust in the Word of God

17

LUKE 1:38 ESV | And Mary said, "Behold, I am the servant of the Lord; let it be to me according to your word." And the angel departed from her.

Consider This

Mary had just received the worst best news of her life. God had highly favored her with a premarital pregnancy, which would be conceived by the Holy Spirit. In other words, she would give birth to the Son of God, and no one would believe it. And she responded with what will be our First Word–Last Word for the day:

"Behold, I am the servant of the Lord; let it be to me according to your word."

A person who says this in the face of difficult news is a consecrated person. In a way, Mary bore the cross before the cross bore her. This is the nature of the consecrated life.

"Behold, I am the servant of the Lord; let it be to me according to your word."

It is the precursor to the prayer her Son Jesus would later pray: "Abba, Father, . . . everything is possible for you. Take this cup from me. Yet not what I will, but what you will" (Mark 14:36).

They are the ultimate words of trusting obedience; words you don't say in considered response to a request because they were already written on your heart long before the request came.

"Behold, I am the servant of the Lord; let it be to me according to your word."

Because we trust God, we have already decided to trust his Word . . . all of it . . . no matter what . . . come what may. It is not an obedient response. It is a preemptive promise. I commend it to you for full-court engagement. It is an everyday Word. Read it aloud. Ruminate over it. Rememberize it. Research it. Rehearse it. Verse it back and forth with others. Make up a tune and sing it. This is a Word that will lead our lives.

"Behold, I am the servant of the Lord; let it be to me according to your word."

First Word. Last Word. God's Word.

The Prayer

Abba Father, behold, I am the servant of the Lord; let it be to me according to your word. I pray in the name of your Son, Jesus. Amen.

The Question

- How might this prayer find its way into the depths of your heart, mind, soul, and strength?

The Word of God Landscapes Our Lives

18

JAMES 1:21 | Therefore, get rid of all moral filth and the evil that is so prevalent and humbly accept the word planted in you, which can save you.

Consider This

We are likely all aware of the law of reaping and sowing. It is straightforward: you reap what you sow. Plant tomatoes; reap tomatoes. Plant zinnias; reap zinnias. So what happens when you plant nothing? Reap nothing? Wrong. Plant nothing; reap weeds.

Isn't that amazing? We get weeds without planting them. They just are. We have two major problems in life: sin and death. They just are. Sin and death are like the weeds of our soul. They are not only present, but prevalent. They suck the life out of us, and they produce nothing of value.

Therefore, get rid of all moral filth and the evil that is so prevalent and humbly accept the word planted in you, which can save you.

Translation: Weed your soul, grow the Word.

Biblical translation: Repent and believe the gospel.

Weeding is a constant challenge. Weeds never give up, and they keep coming back, no matter what. We must stay vigilant and on top of this task or else the weeds will literally take over. More important, though, is what we are sowing and actively growing. In fact, the more the Word of God is growing and bearing fruit in our lives, the more motivated we will be to stay on top of the weeds. Righteousness and love actually have a way of displacing sin and death.

So what does it mean to humbly accept the Word planted in you? I love how James 1:21 is translated in The Message version of the Bible: "So throw all spoiled virtue and cancerous evil in the garbage. In simple humility, let our gardener, God, landscape you with the Word, making a salvation-garden of your life."

To humbly accept the Word planted in us means to surrender to the holy vision of God for our lives. It means deeply engaging God's Word: reading, ruminating, remembering, researching, and rehearsing it. God has a vision and plan for our lives, and we will not know it apart from the Word of God and the Spirit of God. He wills to landscape our lives with his Word, making a salvation-garden of our souls.

Pushing the scriptural metaphor even further, what grows in a salvation-garden? The fruit of the Spirit, of course!— "love, joy, peace, patience, kindness, goodness, faithfulness, gentleness, self-control" (Gal. 5:22–23 ESV).

So throw all spoiled virtue and cancerous evil in the garbage. In simple humility, let our gardener, God, landscape you with the Word, making a salvation-garden of your life. (James 1:21 MSG)

First Word. Last Word. God's Word.

The Prayer

Father, thank you for your Word, which you are always sowing into our lives. I want you to landscape my life with your Word. I want the fruit of the Holy Spirit to grow and flourish in my life. Train me in the discipline of weeding, to pull them from my life at first sight. Even more, give me a compelling vision of your glory for my good. I pray in the name of your Son, Jesus. Amen.

The Questions

- How does this Word resonate with you today? How will you respond to it?

19 The Word of God Is All Light

PSALM 119:105 | **Your word is a lamp for my feet, a light on my path.**

Consider This

Have you ever considered that the first words spoken by God in the Bible are: "Let there be light"? The next four words are even better: "and there was light." But wait! There's more. "God saw that the light was good" (Gen. 1:3–4).

In these few words we see the pattern of all creation and life. God speaks. What he speaks happens. His Word works, accomplishing the purpose for which he sends it. God sees and says it is good. This is the pattern and path for our lives. There is the big problem of sin and death, yet we are freely and extravagantly given the resources of the Word and Spirit, which are to sin and death as light is to darkness.

The Word brings light and life. Sin brings darkness and death. Because of the pervasiveness and prevalence of sin and death, darkness can be a challenge. We need the light of the Word of God in a constant way. It brings us to our First Word–Last Word for today:

Your word is a lamp for my feet, a light on my path.

I remember singing this verse as a song back in the '80s. Because of that oldie-but-goodie Amy Grant melody, I remember-berized it in the good old King James Version, "Thy word is a lamp unto my feet, and a light unto my path." Singing has a way of sowing truth in our hearts, right? The meaning seems straightforward. The Word of God shows us where to walk and where not to walk. As we walk along the paths of our lives, however, we often can't pull out the Bible like a flashlight. The Word will either be in us or not. It's why there is no substitute for the everyday work of living with the Scriptures.

Your word is a lamp for my feet, a light on my path.
First Word. Last Word. God's Word.

The Prayer

Father, thank you for your Word, which not only gives light but is light. Your Word is light from light. Let the brightness of your Word fill and illuminate my soul. Let the light of your Word shine in the still, dim places in my heart and mind. And all of this that my own life might become a living beacon of your light in this world. Thy word is a lamp unto my feet and a light unto my path. May it be so by the power of your Spirit. I pray in the name of your Son, Jesus. Amen.

The Question

- How are you finding the Word of God lighting your path these days?

20 The Word of God Unfolds with Deep Understanding for Simple People

PSALM 119:130 | The unfolding of your words gives light;
it gives understanding to the simple.

Consider This

Psalm 119 is a bit of a party; a comprehensive celebration of the Word of God and the God of the Word. Composed in an acrostic pattern, there are twenty-two sections—one for each letter of the Hebrew alphabet—with eight verses in each section. Coming in at a whopping 176 verses, it is easily the longest chapter in the Bible. We have touched on two other verses from this chapter in this series. Today brings us a third:

The unfolding of your words gives light; it gives under-standing to the simple.

Charles Spurgeon, speaking of Psalm 119, remarked:

> This wonderful psalm, from its great length, helps us to wonder at the immensity of Scripture. From its keeping to one subject it helps us to adore the unity of Scripture; for it is but one. Yet, from the many turns it gives to the same thought, it helps you to see the variety of Scripture. . . . Its variety is that of a kalei-doscope: from a few objects a boundless variation is produced. In the kaleidoscope you look once, and

there is a strangely beautiful form. You shift the glass a very little, and another shape, equally delicate and beautiful, is before your eyes. So it is here.*

The unfolding of your words gives light; it gives understanding to the simple.

Something we can all use more of is simple understanding. Have you considered that as the Word of God opens with the creation, it closes with the new creation? It opens with, "Let there be light" (Gen. 1:3), and it closes with, "And night will be no more. They will need no light of lamp or sun, for the Lord God will be their light, and they will reign forever and ever" (Rev. 22:5 ESV).

The unfolding of your words gives light; it gives understanding to the simple.

There is enormous complexity in almost every aspect of Scripture, yet despite this, it unfolds in a singular story. One simple way of understanding this unfolding of God's Word is to break it into six movements: creation, fall, Israel, Jesus, church, and new creation.

The unfolding of your words gives light; it gives understanding to the simple.

We find ourselves in this unfolding of God's Word right here and right now. We are living in the age of the Spirit, as the people of God, the body of Christ, the church of Jesus Christ. In television parlance, we are in season 5, and in

---

The Complete Works of C. H. Spurgeon, Volume 33, Sermons 1938 to 2000 (Delmarva Publications, Inc., 2013).

order to fully play our part we need to go back and watch seasons 1 through 4 and the previews of season 6 found throughout the whole story and at the end. We must know the settings, the nuances of the characters, the twists and turns of the plot, the cataclysmic climax of the resolution, and how it continues to resolve itself to this present moment and beyond. Who is Naomi and where does she fit? What about Rahab? What is Ezra up to? And what about Nehemiah? Why does Jonah matter? And what about Job? Rachel? Hannah? Every bit of this unfolding Word of God pours more and more understanding into this world of God in which we live out our brief span of days and onward into "the communion of saints, . . . the resurrection of the body, and the life everlasting."

The unfolding of your words gives light; it gives understanding to the simple.

First Word. Last Word. God's Word.

The Prayer

Father, thank you for your Word, which endures forever. Thank you for the way the unfolding of your words gives light and gives understanding to the simple. I don't need a complex grasp of it all. Grant me, a simple person, a simple understanding, which might in time become unfathomably deep. Train me to think in the frames of your story, to have the very mind of Christ, and to live in the marvelous fullness of your Spirit. I pray in the name of your Son, Jesus. Amen.

The Questions

- Which season of the big story do you understand the best? Which do you understand the least?

The Word of God Is Sweet and Bitter (Part 1)

21

EZEKIEL 3:1–3 | And he said to me, "Son of man, eat what is before you, eat this scroll; then go and speak to the people of Israel." So I opened my mouth, and he gave me the scroll to eat. Then he said to me, "Son of man, eat this scroll I am giving you and fill your stomach with it." So I ate it, and it tasted as sweet as honey in my mouth.

Consider This

You are what you eat. We return to this core idea again in today's Daily Text. Twice in today's text we see these three words of command: "Eat this scroll." And the prophet ate it.

Over the last hundred years or so, discipleship has been largely reduced to Christian education, and the coin of the realm in education is study. Study is a good thing, but it can tend to keep us on the outside looking in—dissecting, probing, asking questions, and seeking answers. I do not mean to eschew study (or *research*, as I have called it in our mnemonic device), as I intend to create a larger and more immersive milieu of scriptural engagement in which our study can take deep, transformative roots.

One more brief critique of the status quo. Because the educational paradigm has tended to push discipleship in a more academic direction, we have seen the proliferation of all manner of devotional literature as a kind of corrective. These two different kinds of resources often get pitted against one another. Academics will often eschew devotional material and non-academics can tend to snub academic study resources. Let me say emphatically: this tension between information and inspiration is a false dichotomy.

I don't see the Daily Text as devotional literature, though it designs to catalyze deeper devotion to Jesus Christ. Nor do I see the Daily Text as having an academic agenda, though it aims to teach in ways that inspire deeper digging. My purpose is a full-throated engagement of the text. Any and everything I write intends to point toward a deeper embrace of the Word of God. It's the whole point of this First Word—Last Word—God's Word series. It's why we keep coming back around to the Five-R approach: reading, ruminating, rememberizing, researching, and rehearsing.

For my money, this is how we approach the text on its terms and according to its agenda, which is revelation. The singular agenda of the Word of God is neither to inform nor inspire us, but to reveal the person of God—Father, Son, and Holy Spirit—so we might together enter and embrace a relationship with God in which we might be transformed, recovering the image of God both personally and communally, and all of this to the great and eternal end of the glory of God.

I realize I have digressed a bit today, but I felt it important to exhort you in these ways. It brings us back around to today's text and eating scrolls:

"Then he said to me, 'Son of man, eat this scroll I am giving you and fill your stomach with it.' So I ate it, and it tasted as sweet as honey in my mouth" (Ezek. 3:3).

To eat the Word of God means it must become a comprehensive engagement of our whole lives. Whether you are a skeptical seeker, a new disciple, or a maturing follower of Jesus, the Word of God must become the most central, intentional, focused, and persistent engagement of your life. There is no other way. If you are not eating the Word of God every single day your relationship with God is, at best, anemic and, at worst, a delusion.

You may not appreciate my bluntness here, but you will thank me later. I love you too much to soft-pedal the truth. And the times in which we live are too desperate for a business-as-usual, domesticated religion approach. We need an awakening. We will get the awakening we sow for. It's why we must sow the Word of God near and far, deep and wide, as far as the grace of God will go.

We will get more to the sweet and bitter dimensions of the Word of God tomorrow.

Then he said to me, "Son of man, eat this scroll I am giving you and fill your stomach with it." So I ate it, and it tasted as sweet as honey in my mouth.

First Word. Last Word. God's Word.

The Prayer

Father, thank you for your Word, which endures forever. Wake me up to a deeper way with your Word. I don't want to strive for more but to surrender deeper. I don't want to raise the level of my commitment but to deepen my consecration to you. I want your Word to become my world. I want to hunger for your Word and thirst for your Spirit. I want more than anything for your Word to take deep root in my soul, restoring me to the image of God, enlarging my capacity to know you and represent you in this world. Increase my appetite for your Word, Lord. I pray in the name of your Son, Jesus. Amen.

The Questions

- What is "business as usual" for you when it comes to God's Word? What might the next level look like? How might you take a step into that today?

22 The Word of God Is Sweet and Bitter (Part 2)

REVELATION 10:9–10 | So I went to the angel and asked him to give me the little scroll. He said to me, "Take it and eat it. It will turn your stomach sour, but 'in your mouth it will be as sweet as honey.'" I took the little scroll from the angel's hand and ate it. It tasted as sweet as honey in my mouth, but when I had eaten it, my stomach turned sour.

Consider This

In yesterday's text, the prophet Ezekiel was commanded to "eat this scroll" (Ezek. 3:3) and upon doing so he found it tasted sweeter than honey. Today we see something similar yet with a key difference, as the revelation given to John unfolds:

It tasted as sweet as honey in my mouth, but when I had eaten it, my stomach turned sour.

Sometimes, the Word of God can be like this; sweet to the taste yet bitter to the stomach. It can taste sweeter than honey and yet have the effect of medicine in our bodies. We commonly hear from cancer patients how chemotherapy makes them sick before making them better. Are we open to this kind of experience with the Word of God?

Early this past summer I was sharing with a group of college students, asking them to share particular scriptures that were presently living and active in their lives. One of them shared this word from the prophet Habakkuk:

> Though the fig tree does not bud
>> and there are no grapes on the vines,
> though the olive crop fails
>> and the fields produce no food,
> though there are no sheep in the pen
>> and no cattle in the stalls,
> yet I will rejoice in the LORD,
> I will be joyful in God my Savior.
>
> The Sovereign LORD is my strength;
>> he makes my feet like the feet of a deer,
>> he enables me to tread on the heights. (Hab. 3:17–19)

I had heard the text before, but it struck me differently this time. The past several years had been a very difficult season in the life of my family. That scripture whispered hope to me in the midst of my despair, particularly the closing verses about ascending to the heights. For the next several days I ruminated on the text, writing it each morning in my journal. Soon I had it rememberized. I started researching Habakkuk to learn more of how it fit within the larger biblical story.

About midway through the summer, as I engaged these verses, I sensed the Lord speaking to me. The Holy Spirit made me aware of my failure to rehearse this word from the Lord. If you were to peruse my summer journal you would see how I began to abbreviate the Scripture: "No figs. No grapes. No olives. No grain. No sheep. No cows. Yet I will rejoice in the Lord." While the nos gripped my sense of reality, the invitation to rejoice eluded my experience. I would read the words, but they rang hollow in my soul. I sensed the Lord inquiring of me, "You are waiting for things to get better, aren't you? You are waiting to rejoice in me until your circumstances and conditions improve and you get past this dark valley."

It tasted as sweet as honey in my mouth, but when I had eaten it, my stomach turned sour.

Indigestion was setting in. I was comfortable commiserating with the prophet in his despair yet I resisted the move to rejoice in the Lord in the midst of it. I would rejoice when the Lord lifted the pain. The leading of the Spirit impressed upon me, "Now is the time to rejoice, in the midst of the ruins; not after they are somehow repaired. This is that moment for you, John David. Rejoice in the Lord in the ruins. Do not miss this moment."

It tasted as sweet as honey in my mouth, but when I had eaten it, my stomach turned sour.

Talk about a sour stomach. My heart, mind, and spirit were in unfamiliar, very difficult terrain. This was gut-level pain. I was comfortable with a despairing response to despairing conditions. Rejoicing in God in the face of them was utterly foreign to me. I would rejoice when he lifted them. "No," he said, "now is the time."

"I will rejoice in the LORD, I will be joyful in God my Savior" (Hab. 3:18). The words themselves began to train my will. As I obeyed, I began to discover the next verse in my experience, "The Sovereign LORD is my strength" (Hab. 3:19). I was ready to move on to the last two verses about him making my feet like the feet of a deer and taking me back to the mountaintop. The Lord chided me to stay with rejoicing at the bottom. The rest would come in his timing, not mine.

I would like to tell you that I am back on top, with bumper crops and mountaintop joy now. I am not. I am still learning the lesson of the valley—to rejoice in the ruins. It continues to be the hardest learning of my life so far. Every single day, in the bitterness of loss, like the dripping medicine of a chemotherapy IV, he infuses me with the invitation, "Yet I will rejoice in the LORD, I will be joyful in God my Savior" (Hab. 3:18). Slowly, I sense the malignant cancer of a despairing spirit begin to dissipate. I am growing stronger in the Lord. I will ascend in his time, not by clawing and climbing my way out, but as he lifts me up to himself.

It tasted as sweet as honey in my mouth, but when I had eaten it, my stomach turned sour.

First Word. Last Word. God's Word.

The Prayer

Father, thank you for your Word, which endures forever. Thank you for making it like medicine when we most need it. You graciously coat the bitter pill with sugar that we might swallow it, and yet you do not spare us of the souring effects of its healing. Lead me to these kinds of words that I might eat them, without fear of the side effects, because I know you are making me well, ridding me of the sickness of sin and death and imbuing me with your very nature. I pray in the name of your Son, Jesus. Amen.

The Questions

- Can you think of a time when you experienced the Word of God like medicine? Perhaps sweet to the taste yet sour in the stomach? Do you sense this need in your life now? Ask him for such a word.

The Word of God Is like Fire in Our Hearts and in Our Bones

23

JEREMIAH 20:9 | But if I say, "I will not mention his word
   or speak anymore in his name,"
his word is in my heart like a fire,
   a fire shut up in my bones.
I am weary of holding it in;
   indeed, I cannot.

Consider This

If there is anything we are learning in this series, it is the deeply engaging, personally invasive nature of the Word of God. We eat it like bread. It tastes sweeter than honey. It can turn sour in the stomach. Like a surgical double-edged knife it pierces and penetrates to the inaccessible places of our inner life. It teaches, corrects, rebukes, and trains us in righteousness. It landscapes our souls.

Today brings us to yet another deeply interior impact of the Word of God:

His word is in my heart like a fire, a fire shut up in my bones.

Jeremiah was something of a prophet's prophet. He was a master of the prophetic gesture; his life became the signs he prophesied. He had to say many hard things to God's people concerning their own idolatry, their neglect of the people in need all around them, and the coming judgment of God in response to their callous rebellion. This gap between the word Jeremiah received from God and what he witnessed in the world led him to describe his reality as follows:

His word is in my heart like a fire, a fire shut up in my bones. I am weary of holding it in; indeed, I cannot.

The Word of God was in Jeremiah, and the Spirit of God was on him. While we may not be called in the unique way of Jeremiah, as a prophet, we are all called to be fed by the Word and led by the Spirit. Over time, the cumulative effect of this kind of life and lifestyle is that of becoming a signpost of revelation ourselves; a touchpoint of the transcendence of God; bushes on fire yet not being consumed. I like the way Paul puts it in 2 Corinthians 4:7: "But we have this treasure in jars of clay to show that this all-surpassing power is from God and not from us."

His word is in my heart like a fire, a fire shut up in my bones.

Several years ago I found myself in church on a Sunday morning listening to an intriguing message from a Jewish scholar, a professor at a highly noteworthy Christian seminary. Her teaching exuded a winsome mixture of plausibility and polish that had everyone leaning forward in their seats. Because she was a professor of the New Testament, people assumed she was a Christian. As a New Testament scholar, she said many true and helpful things, and yet something in my spirit was firing up. She was speaking of Jesus in ways truthful yet woefully incomplete, and she was clearly winning followers. I began to experience what Jeremiah was talking about in today's text:

His word is in my heart like a fire, a fire shut up in my bones.

I knew I had to do something. But what? There were easily a thousand people in the room. I felt the pain Jeremiah referenced when he said:

I am weary of holding it in; indeed, I cannot.

As she neared the end of her presentation, she asked if anyone wanted to pose a question. By this point, I was a full-blown burning bush in my seat. I stood up and, in the most respectful tone, asked the professor this question: "Do you believe that Jesus Christ was physically raised from the dead?" You could have heard a pin drop in the large room. She stood in what seemed like a stunned silence, and then she answered with a single word, "No." You could hear an audible gasp across the room. I thought to my lawyerly self, *No further questions, your honor.* I sat down.

his word is in my heart like a fire, a fire shut up in my bones. I am weary of holding it in; indeed, I cannot.

First Word. Last Word. God's Word.

The Prayer

Father, thank you for your Word, which endures forever. Thank you for this witness from your prophet, Jeremiah. I want for your Word to be in my heart like a fire, a fire shut up in my bones. Kindle this fire in me. Make of my heart a fireplace for your Word and Spirit to burn with a passion to love you and a purpose to do your will. Give me courage to share it with grace and boldness and with even more humility. I pray in the name of your Son, Jesus. Amen.

The Questions
- Have you or are you experiencing the Word of God in your heart like a fire, a fire shut up in your bones? Will you ask the Holy Spirit to grow this reality in you?

24 The Words of God and the Word of God (Part 1)

LUKE 24:32 | They asked each other, "Were not our hearts burning within us while he talked with us on the road and opened the Scriptures to us?"

Consider This
Today we make the turn and enter the stretch run on this First Word—Last Word—God's Word series. We will hone our focus on the Word of God by fixing our gaze on the second person of the Trinity, Jesus Christ.

Let's begin with an affirmation: We read Scripture with, in, through, for, and because of Jesus. Because most all of us are Gentiles, apart from Jesus, we would likely have no awareness of Scripture, much less familiarity. We read Scripture as Christians—the followers of Jesus, under the inspiration of the Holy Spirit, through our participation in the church, and in fellowship with the communion of saints.

Jesus is the subject, object, and the verbiage of the movement of Scripture. Consider our First Word–Last Word text for today:

They asked each other, "Were not our hearts burning within us while he talked with us on the road and opened the Scriptures to us?"

Our understanding of and love for the words of Scripture depend on our life with the Word, who is Jesus. Consider the context of today's text. It is evening on the day of resurrection. Two dejected disciples of Jesus are walking from Jerusalem to Emmaus, discussing the disaster of the death of Jesus, and this happens: "As they talked and discussed these things with each other, Jesus himself came up and walked along with them" (Luke 24:15). Whether intended or not, we see a beautiful allusion to Deuteronomy 6:7: "'Talk about them when you sit at home and when you walk along the road, when you lie down and when you get up.'"

As they explained to Jesus (whom they didn't recognize) all that had happened, he said this,

> 'How foolish you are, and how slow to believe all that the prophets have spoken! Did not the Messiah have to suffer these things and then enter his glory?' And beginning with Moses and all the Prophets, he explained to them what was said in all the Scriptures concerning himself. (Luke 24:25–27)

We tend to think of the Scriptures (the Old Testament, in this case) and Jesus as two different things. In fact, we tend to have a fairly derivative understanding of Jesus altogether. Our knowledge of Jesus is sourced by doctrine, Sunday school, our experiences—for better or worse, folk religion, culture, and yes, Scripture. Only the Holy Spirit can sort all this out for us. This encounter on the road to Emmaus gives us a glimpse of what it looks like when this happens.

These disciples who walked along the road knew the Scriptures, and they had some kind of relationship with Jesus, but these were two somewhat separate things in their minds. They had not properly understood the Scriptures and, hence, they had not properly understood Jesus. Then "beginning with Moses and all the Prophets, he explained to them what was said in all the Scriptures concerning himself" (v. 27).

As they came to Emmaus, they invited him to dine with them. "When he was at the table with them, he took bread, gave thanks, broke it and began to give it to them. Then their eyes were opened and they recognized him, and he disappeared from their sight" (vv. 30–31).

Finally, after Jesus disappeared, the disciples offered this reflection:

They asked each other, "Were not our hearts burning within us while he talked with us on the road and opened the Scriptures to us?"

The Scriptures and Jesus can be two different things, yet unless they become for us one Holy Spirit–filled, seamless reality we will miss them both. We cannot understand Jesus apart from the Scriptures, and we will not understand the Scriptures apart from Jesus. We will pick up there tomorrow.

They asked each other, "Were not our hearts burning within us while he talked with us on the road and opened the Scriptures to us?"

First Word. Last Word. God's Word.

The Prayer

Father, thank you for your Word, which endures forever. Thank you for your words as we have them in the Scriptures. Thank you for your Word you have given us in your Son. And thank you for your Spirit who reveals the Word who is your Son by the words which are your Scriptures; and who interprets the words of Scripture through the Word, our Teacher, who is your Son. Lead us into this place where our hearts burn within us, even at the thought of your Word. Lead us to this place where we walk along the road with Jesus and one another and talk about such things. More of Jesus. More of your Word. More of your Spirit. I pray in the name of your Son, Jesus. Amen.

The Question

• Does today's text and reflection feel more like a circular riddle to you or does it help make the relationship between the Word and the words of Scripture more clear and understandable?

25 The Words of God and the Word of God (Part 2)

JOHN 1:1–5 | In the beginning was the Word, and the Word was with God, and the Word was God. He was with God in the beginning. Through him all things were made; without him nothing was made that has been made. In him was life, and that life was the light of all mankind. The light shines in the darkness, and the darkness has not overcome it.

Consider This

In the beginning was the Word . . .

There are the words of God and there is the Word of God, but let's be clear about something: the words of God in Scripture, as in every single word, are the Word of God. Scripture does not contain God's Word. Scripture *is* God's Word. Full stop, period. And because Holy Scripture is the Word of God it is authoritative. It carries the authority of the author, who is Father, Son, and Holy Spirit.

. . . and the Word was with God,

This is one of the most fundamental and foundational doctrines of our faith. Despite all manner of heretical scholarship and false teaching concerning Holy Scripture that has arisen from the earliest days of the church to the present day, it remains the uncompromised, unscathed, and unassailably authoritative Word of God. We do not sit in judgment over the Word of God. The Word of God sits in judgment over us.

. . . and the Word was God.

There are the words of God which are the Word of God and then there is the Word of God who is the person of God himself, God the Son, the second person of the Trinity.

He was with God in the beginning.

Let's rehearse again the affirmation we began with yesterday: We read Scripture with, in, through, for, and because of Jesus. We read Scripture as Christians—the followers of Jesus, under the inspiration of the Holy Spirit, through our participation in the body of Christ—the church, and in fellowship with the communion of saints.

Through him all things were made; without him nothing was made that has been made.

The Word of God created the world by speaking the words of God, and from nothing came everything. Hear the words of God through the inspired apostolic voice of Paul to the Colossians:

> The Son is the image of the invisible God, the firstborn over all creation. For in him all things were created: things in heaven and on earth, visible and invisible, whether thrones or powers or rulers or authorities; all things have been created through him and for him. He is before all things, and in him all things hold together. (Col. 1:15–17)

The Word of God, who is the image of God, fashioned human beings in his very image, male and female, and breathed into us the breath of life.

In him was life, and that life was the light of all mankind.

Light and life—this is the essence of the Creator and the creation, and we see them perfectly manifest in the creative genius of the Word of God through this marvelous articulation of the words of God:

In the beginning was the Word, and the Word was with God, and the Word was God. He was with God in the beginning. Through him all things were made; without him nothing was made that has been made. In him was life, and that life was the light of all mankind. The light shines in the darkness, and the darkness has not overcome it.

First Word. Last Word. God's Word.

The Prayer

Father, thank you for your Word, which endures forever. Thank you for the preexistence of your Word; before anything ever was you were. Thank you for your Son, who is the Word of God, who is the image of the invisible God—the exact representation of your being. And thank you that all things hold together in the Word of God. Thank you for the way your Spirit helps us to grasp these incomprehensible mysteries and to marvel at them. There is nothing to do but stand in awe and bow in worship. We pray in the name of your Son, Jesus. Amen.

The Questions

- Can you get to a place of wonder and awe at the majesty of these revelations from the words of God concerning the Word of God? Do they fill your heart and mind with a spirit of worship? If not, ask for this to be the case.

The Words of God and the Word of God (Part 3)

26

JOHN 1:14–18 | The Word became flesh and made his dwelling among us. We have seen his glory, the glory of the one and only Son, who came from the Father, full of grace and truth.

(John testified concerning him. He cried out, saying, "This is the one I spoke about when I said, 'He who comes after me has surpassed me because he was before me.'") Out of his fullness we have all received grace in place of grace already given. For the law was given through Moses; grace and truth came through Jesus Christ. No one has ever seen God, but the one and only Son, who is himself God and is in closest relationship with the Father, has made him known.

Consider This

It is impossible to overestimate the revolutionary impact of these four words:

The Word became flesh.

The eternal Word of God, the preexistent Son of God, the second person of the Trinity became a human being. The uncreated Creator became a begotten creature—conceived by the Holy Spirit, fully God; born of the virgin Mary, fully human:

The Word became flesh.

Let's return to this cosmic creed Paul gave to the Colossians: "For God was pleased to have all his fullness dwell in him, and through him to reconcile to himself all things, whether things on earth or things in heaven, by making peace through his blood, shed on the cross" (Col. 1:19–20).

Because of the enormous gravity of verse 20 and its immediate impact on our lives, we can tend to miss the miraculous implications of verse 19: "For God was pleased to have all his fullness dwell in him." Say that aloud: "For God was pleased to have all his fullness dwell in him." They amplify the four words with which we began:

The Word became flesh.

All the energy over the last hundred years or so has gone into leading people to believe in Jesus, the importance of which I do not wish to diminish. The trouble is we have settled into a transactional understanding of Jesus and the gospel. To be sure, there is a transactional dimension—his righteousness for our sin, his suffering for our salvation, his death for our life. John 3:16 couldn't be more clear: "For God so loved the world that he gave his one and only Son, that whoever believes in him shall not perish but have eternal life."

The gospel has a transactional dimension, but the minute the gospel is reduced to a transaction is the minute it becomes something less than the gospel. Notice also the thrust of John 1:12 couldn't be clearer: "Yet to all who did receive him, to those who believed in his name, he gave the right to become children of God."

We have focused on the eternal part and neglected the life part. We have emphasized believing and short-sold becoming. We have championed getting people into heaven while forgetting about getting heaven into people. The gospel of Jesus Christ is not a transaction. It is an invitation to the kind of transformation that leads to a transcendent life—the glorious spectacle of real holiness.

The Word became flesh and made his dwelling among us.

This is so in order that the Word might become flesh in our own lives and communities. See how Paul weaves this same story with the Colossians:

> I have become its servant by the commission God gave me to present to you the word of God in its fullness—the mystery that has been kept hidden for ages and generations, but is now disclosed to the Lord's people. To them God has chosen to make known among the Gentiles the glorious riches of this mystery, which is Christ in you, the hope of glory. (Col. 1:25–27)

The eternal Word of God, Jesus Christ, in you—in me—for others, this is the gospel. This is the Word of God in its fullness. This is the transformation that leads to transcendence; a life of beholding the Son of God, which becomes a life in which the Son of God can be received, believed, and beheld by others. This is how the glory of God is revealed.

The Word became flesh and made his dwelling among us. We have seen his glory, the glory of the one and only Son, who came from the Father, full of grace and truth.

First Word. Last Word. God's Word.

The Prayer

Father, thank you for your Word, which endures forever. Thank you for these four words that changed everything: *The Word became flesh.* This is such good news! And I know that as this same Word of God dwells in me I, too, become good news. Transcend my flesh with the glory of your presence that my ordinary life may become a place for your extraordinary love. Forgive me for settling for anything less. I pray in the name of your Son, Jesus. Amen.

The Questions

Do you believe it is possible for the Word to become flesh in your life? Why or why not? Think of a time when you have experienced this. How might you experience this more?

27 The Words of God and the Word of God (Part 4)

JOHN 5:39–40 | You study the Scriptures diligently because you think that in them you have eternal life. These are the very Scriptures that testify about me, yet you refuse to come to me to have life.

Consider This

We have spent every day for a month now extolling the extraordinary value and virtue of the Scriptures as the Word of God. What I am about to say may seem contradictory, yet it is not. I say it at the risk of undermining everything I have written. You know my regard for Scripture, the Word of God, which over these past few days I have referred to as the words of God. You know also my love for Jesus, the Word of God, about whom, in whom, and through whom we have the words of God. So rather than me saying the apparently contradictory thing, let's ask Jesus to say it:

You study the Scriptures diligently because you think that in them you have eternal life. These are the very Scriptures that testify about me, yet you refuse to come to me to have life.

Here's the overstated emphatic translation for which I am sometimes congratulated and other times chided: apart from Jesus, the words of Scripture are worthless. Our life does not come from a book. Our life comes from God: Father, Son, and Holy Spirit.

Jesus is speaking here to Pharisees, people who fanatically revered the Scriptures and who knew them upside down. They loved the Law and the Prophets like nobody's business. In fact, keeping the Law to the absolute letter *was* their business. With this declaration, Jesus, in essence, declared their business bankrupt.

There is a way of revering the Bible that completely misses the point of the Bible. There is a way of exalting and even obeying the words of God that defy the God of the Word. Hear Jesus out: "And the Father who sent me has himself testified concerning me. You have never heard his voice nor seen his form, nor does his word dwell in you, for you do not believe the one he sent" (John 5:37–38).

While we do not know Jesus apart from the Bible, we cannot understand the Bible apart from Jesus. Broadly speaking, there are three kinds of people: There are those who want the Bible without Jesus and those who want Jesus without the Bible. (I will deal with the third kind shortly.)

Those who want the Bible without Jesus still believe in Jesus. They salute him. They consider themselves the leading Christians, and they come off with a kind of rigorous certainty in all matters of doctrine, faith, and practice. They are classic legalists and, in most cases, they have no idea of it.

Those who want Jesus without the Bible still believe in the Bible. They consider themselves the enlightened Christians who understand Jesus so well, they can disregard much of the Old Testament and most of Paul as being "bound by its culture and time." They take license with the Bible. The former group wants to control by exalting the Scripture. The latter group wants to accommodate by setting the Scripture aside.

Both groups miss the whole picture and point. They get neither the words of God nor the Word of God. They don't understand the Bible or Jesus because they have learned a way of revering one at the cost of the other. In other words, one group makes an idol of the Bible, and the other makes an idol out of Jesus. And, yes, they have no idea of it, which makes sense because it is the very nature of an idol to make its adherent like itself—which is to say blind, deaf, and hard-hearted. Taking on either of these groups will get you crucified. Just ask Jesus.

This is where Jesus comes in and turns over the tables on the whole party. Remember this word from yesterday: "The Word became flesh and made his dwelling among us. We have seen his glory, the glory of the one and only Son, who came from the Father, full of grace and truth" (John 1:14).

Truth is not truth without grace, and grace is not grace without truth. They are two sides of the same coin; a unified and indissoluble dimension of reality only found in the person and presence of Jesus Christ—God incarnate. Truth and grace are not two things that need to be held in balance or, worse, tension. They are one thing. In fact, they are not a thing. Grace and Truth are a person, or they are nothing. They are a community (i.e., the body of Christ), or they are meaningless words and ideals.

It brings us to the third kind of person: the ones who love the Word of God and the words of God with an undivided heart. These people are those in whom the Word is becoming flesh; those who are filled with the fullness of grace and truth. This third kind of person is a mature and maturing Christian, for whom the Word of God and the words of God live in seamless union. Their lives defy classification into the thin categories of the world because they have learned to live in the world possessed by a transcendent holiness both arresting and awe-inspiring.

You study the Scriptures diligently because you think that in them you have eternal life. These are the very Scriptures that testify about me, yet you refuse to come to me to have life.

First Word. Last Word. God's Word.

The Prayer

Father, thank you for your Word, which endures forever. Thank you for your Word, the eternal Son of God. To know him is to know eternal life. Forgive us for our idolatrous ways and show us the way to true repentance, which is to whole-heartedly embrace Jesus Christ. Thank you for this one who is full of grace and truth. Let our lives be filled with his life, for then we will be filled with grace and truth. I pray in the name of your Son, Jesus. Amen.

The Questions

- Have you encountered or observed examples of the three kinds of people mentioned in today's Daily Text? Which of the three kinds of people are you? In which way do you tend to err?

28 First Word. Last Word. God's Word.—Final Word

PSALM 18:30 | As for God, his way is perfect:
The Lord's word is flawless;
he shields all who take refuge in him.

Consider This

Back when we lived in Texas, we visited Lakewood Church from time to time in its pre-arena neighborhood. The late

John Osteen (Joel's father) always began his message by inviting the people to lift up their Bibles in the air and recite a short creed with him:

> I am what it says I am.
> I can do what it says I can do.
> Today, I will be taught the Word of God.
> I boldly confess:
> My mind is alert, my heart is receptive.
> I will never be the same.
> I am about to receive the incorruptible, indestructible,
>   ever-living seed of the Word of God.
> I will never be the same.
> Never, never, never.
> I will never be the same.
> In Jesus' name. Amen.

Ever since then I have wanted to write a Bible Creed. It seems fitting as we end the First Word—Last Word—God's Word series to take a crack at it. Without further adieu, here it is:

I believe in the living Word of God,
  who is the Son of God, Jesus Christ.

And I believe in the written Word of God, the Bible,
  the Holy Spirit–inspired authority of the people of God.

God's Word endures forever,
  is sweeter than honey,
  more precious than gold,

sharper than a double-edged sword,
judging the thoughts and attitudes of the heart.

This Word is perfect, trustworthy, right,
radiant, pure, firm, and flawless.
It refreshes the soul,
makes wise the simple,
gives joy to the heart,
is a lamp to my feet and a light to my path.

God's Word teaches, corrects, rebukes, and trains.
It cleanses and prunes, feeds and nourishes,
is purposeful and powerful.
It burns like a fire in my bones.
It always accomplishes the purposes for which it is sent.

God's Word will be on my heart,
on my gate, on my doorpost.
I will talk about it when I lie down and
when I wake up and when I walk along the road.
I will read, ruminate, rememberize, research, and rehearse it,
building my life on the rock of God's Word.
Indeed, "the grass withers and the flowers fall,
but the word of our God endures forever."

It will be the first Word.
It will be the last Word.
This is God's Word.*

---

*This poem is inspired by Scripture. See the following verses: John 1:1, 2 Timothy 3:16–17, Isaiah 40:8, Psalm 19:10, Hebrews 4:12, Psalm 19:7–9, Psalm 199:105, John 15:2–8, Isaiah 55:8–9, 11, Jeremiah 20:9, Deuteronomy 6:4–9.

The Prayer

Father, thank you for your Word. May it become my life. I pray in the name of your Son, Jesus, the Word made flesh. Amen.

The Questions

What stands out to you about this series? How will you take it forward?